Around the Table

Leadership Lessons from The Summit

ISBN: 978-1-990784-04-0

Summit Global Publishing Ltd.
info@summitglobalpublishing.ca

Edited by: Tracy Belford, Tamar Smith, Barbara Bearht

Cover by: Jocelyn Pinzon

Bible References

Scripture quotations marked KJV are taken from **The Holy Bible: King James Version.** (1995). (electronic ed. of the 1769 edition of the 1611 Authorized Version., Ps 51:6). Bellingham WA: Logos Research Systems, Inc. Used by permission

Scripture quotations marked NIV are taken from **The Holy Bible: New International Version.** (1984). Grand Rapids, MI: Zondervan. Used by permission

Scripture quotations marked TPT are taken from **The Passion Translation®**. Copyright © 2017, 2018, 2020 by Passion & Fire Ministries, Inc. Used by permission. All rights reserved. ThePassionTranslation.com.

Scripture quotations marked NESB are taken from **The Holy Bible, English Standard Version®**), copyright © 2001 by Crossway, a publishing ministry of Good News Publishers. Used by permission. All rights reserved.

Scripture quotations marked NLT are taken from **Holy Bible, New Living Translation**, Copyright © 1996, 2004, 2015 by Tyndale House Foundation. Used by permission of Tyndale House Publishers, Inc., Carol Stream, Illinois 60188. All rights reserved.

Scripture quotations marked NKJV are taken from **New King James Version**. Copyright © 1982 by Thomas Nelson, Inc. Used by permission. All rights reserved.

Scripture quotations marked AMP are taken from **Amplified® Bible** (AMP) Copyright © 2015 by The Lockman Foundation. Used by permission. www.Lockman.org.

Scripture quotations marked NHEB are from the **New Heart English Bible.** No permissions needed.

Around the Table

Leadership Lessons from The Summit

Compiled by Tracy Belford

Dedication

This book has been in my heart for a long time. Every week I am surrounded by world class leaders as we sit together and determine how to steer this ship that we call The Summit. For this reason, I dedicate this book to my fellow co-workers in the gospel, the staff of The Summit Edmonton Church. You are, without a doubt, anointed, called, and set apart.

Acknowledgements

Thank you to all our staff at The Summit Edmonton Church. I value the words of wisdom I have gained as we sat together at the table. You have all changed me deeply.

For these devotions, I want to thank specifically:

Des Belford, the love of my life
Chris Mathis
Nikki Mathis
Jamie Paton
Heather Paton
TJ Green
Chris Frost
Paulina Guinez
Krysta Koppel
Rebekah Ryzuk

There are others around the table whose devotions I have not included in this book like Wendy Leigh, Angel Sanders, and Heather Bernard, who are so very valuable to our team, as well as the others who have sat around the table over the years.

All your contributions have helped us to become the leaders we are today.

Foreword

When I began my journey into publishing, this book was already stirring in me. Each week at The Summit Edmonton Church, we have a staff meeting around a table. Around this table, we are all different—we have different positions and strengths. We each have value, we each contribute, and we come together as a team. Some of us are pastors, some are administrators, some are children's ministers, and some are audio visual technicians. None of those things diminish or elevate our status on the team.

I wanted to publish this book about our table because it has been so empowering to sit together; each of us is rising up because of the greatness of the others at the table. We inspire one another on to greater work for the Kingdom.

Long ago, Dean Briggs came to our table and spoke to us about keeping our table clean. It meant we needed to keep short accounts with each other, forgiving quickly when occasions arise.

Sitting around the table together is sometimes messy. Sometimes we make messes with each other that we have to clean up. We strive to keep short accounts with the Lord and with each other. But that is the beauty of the table.

Each week, we start out with worship, then one of us takes a turn leading a devotion, which comes with a question that we all wrestle with together, followed by a time of testimonies, and then we get down to business.

Because we take turns leading the devotions, the devotions are incredibly varied, based on the strengths of each team member, as well as what each person is walking through in the moment.

These devotions have been an incredible source of growth for each of us, as well as a place of vulnerability, where the ensuing discussions have brought us into deep places together. They have brought unity, and they have challenged our hearts. My hope and prayer is that they also challenge you, and that you will use them to go further and higher than we have, to walk in revival, and to reach your city for Jesus Christ.

We are one body in Christ, and just as we have learned and grown from each other, I pray that you also learn and grow from reading this book.

Tracy Belford

Table of Contents

Lesson 1 Maturity 1

Lesson 2 Building the House of God 9

Lesson 3 Team Growth 21

Lesson 4 The Cost of Discipleship 29

Lesson 5 The Wine is Worth the Wait 35

Lesson 6 Deliverance 39

Lesson 7 Creativity 45

Lesson 8 Old Testament vs New Testament 49

Lesson 9 Managing Our Inner Man 55

Lesson 10 Stop and Sit by the Well 67

Lesson 11 Identity 71

Lesson 12 When You Succeed at Your Life's Call 75

Lesson 13 Time Management 79

Lesson 14 I Wanna Be Me, Not You 85

Lesson 15 Empowerment & Development 89

Lesson 16 The Business of Revival 95

Lesson 17 Going Through the Fire with Jesus 101

Lesson 18 Hard Truths 107

Lesson 19 Living with the Robe of the Lastborn 115

Lesson 20 Small Moves That Have a Big Impact 125

Lesson 21 A Sound Mind 131

Lesson 22 Legacy 137

Lesson 23 Marriage 141

Lesson 24 The Busyness of Life 149
Lesson 25 Come as a Child 153
Lesson 26 Rejection & Abandonment.............................. 159
Lesson 27 Sight vs Vision... 165
Lesson 28 God as Father 167
Lesson 29 Jesus Style Leadership 173
Lesson 30 Bloom 181
Lesson 31 Loyal Love... 189
Lesson 32 Season of Rebuilding 195
Lesson 33 Valuing One Another 203
Lesson 34 Pioneering and Church Growth 207
Lesson 35 Mantles 213
Lesson 36 Church Leadership 221

Lesson 1 Maturity

TJ Green

Maturity has been one of the cries of my heart. I have been praying that God would mature me to produce fruit this year. I want to be transformed into the image of Jesus. Maturity is one of the things that we can control.

I was talking to my son, Dax, one morning on the way to school and I told him, "Someone who has self-control is going to be a highly successful individual. They're going to be happy in life, and because of delayed gratification, they are going to be gratified more. Like when they get their school breakfast ready the night before instead of rushing in the morning. More than that, even though they only want to play video games, they can tell themselves they are going to prepare for tomorrow, then tomorrow becomes a better day." My son has seen that practically in these little moments.

Self-control is something I feel God is growing in me. I was thinking about Esau and Jacob and how Esau's momentary craving caused him to despise his birthright. He came back from the country and was hungry, and his craving made him say, "I'm going to die. My birthright means nothing to me." His craving was so strong that his birthright meant nothing to him! How many times in my life has the momentary craving meant more than something eternal in my life? Esau sold his birthright to Jacob for a bowl of beans, as Jacob would do anything for the birthright.

I'm inspired by people who are highly driven and disciplined with their health, fitness, and life. I'm not naturally that way, but I always aspire to be. When I'm driving and I see people running, I say, "I respect that." I'm not doing it, but I respect it.

It's interesting to look at self-control. Have you ever thought about what self-control looks like in heaven?

Jesus was the perfect example of love. He was God in the flesh. So, He was perfectly self-controlled. He was the only person ever on Earth who walked in perfect self-control. Yet, He was accused of being a wine bibber and a glutton. So obviously, self-control looks different in heaven than what a human understanding looks like. It's being so free from vices and cravings of the flesh that you get to enjoy life to the fullest because you're full of God and you're enjoying life with God.

Mature Christians are self-controlled. Another way you can think of it is "Spirit-led". *For those who are led by the Spirit of God are the children of God. Romans 8:14 NIV* Christians are self-controlled or Spirit-led.

Mature Christians change their minds or are humble enough to keep learning or hang on to Jesus more than their worldview or theology. They are allowed to change. They keep growing because they don't get stuck in a rut. That's maturity. My theory is that my theology is constantly changing because of encountering Jesus. Every time I encounter Jesus; I hope to see Him in a way that I've never seen Him before. My theology must make room for that. Your theology should be consistently growing and changing. You should be hanging on to Jesus more than your worldview or more than your theology.

I think one of the biggest struggles every preacher or church leader has is to share God's Word, but not through the lens of their own soul. Many times, you start to interpret theology, or the Word of God, through the lens of your own soul.

I was mentored by a man who was very Calvinistic. When I understood his story, I understood why he needed to think God was this way. It brought him security in life because God was consistent. God never changed, God predestined everything, God was in control, and this man had that view because it gave him security. His theology about God was entrenched, but it gave his soul some comfort. Many times, we can interpret the Scripture through a lens of past hurts.

I think about some of the dangerous doctrines of the world like deconstruction. It can be a good thing and a bad thing, but really it is a theology that comes from a place of hurt. Our story becomes more important than His story. How many times have we made our feelings into our story or our opinion, and then try to approach God that way; or fix refined Scriptures to reinforce our already made-up minds because of our pasts and our journey?

I think mature Christians change their minds; mature Christians repent. They say, "God, I thought this way about You. I thought this way about life but now I change my mind."

What's the mind of Christ? When we are willing to learn, we are willing to grow in our view of God. When we get married to doctrine or theology, it can be easy to start digging a ditch. We can get entrenched in our opinion, but I believe that's a sign of immaturity, that we trust more in our own beliefs about God than God Himself. Unless we've arrived, which nobody has, I think it's healthy to have a suspicion about our own opinions, our own worldview, or even our own theology and thoughts about God.

Apostle Paul talks about adding to or taking away from Scripture. And he goes as far to say: *But even if we or an angel from heaven should preach a gospel other than the one we preached to you, let them be under God's curse! As we have already said, so now I say again: If anybody is preaching to you a gospel other than what you accepted, let them be under God's curse! Galatians 1:8-9 NIV*

I warn everyone who hears the words of the prophecy of this book: if anyone adds to them, God will add to him the plagues described in this book, and if anyone takes away from the words of the book of this prophecy, God will take away his share in the tree of life and in the holy city, which are described in this book. Revelation 22:8-19 ESV

When we add to the work, it's our own religion, and because of this, we are now coming under the curse. I've experienced times I've added to the Word where I put a lens between the Word and what I've experienced. I think God wants to give us his corrective lenses. We all need corrective lenses.

We need Jesus to be our vision. It's Christ being the center. Religion will always want to complicate things and add things to it. It's Jesus "plus".

"If you do this, you'll get this result." But Paul said to preach Christ and Christ crucified. The power of the Holy Spirit is when you preach the death, burial, and the resurrection of Jesus. The simplicity of the gospel is also the power of the gospel.

Mature Christians have the courage to change their minds or repent or receive the mind of Christ.

I believe churches should stop pointing out everyone else's sin and start with personal responsibility. I heard a Bible professor once say he knew he was experiencing a fresh touch of God when he stopped confessing everyone else's sin and started confessing his own. Dwight L. Moody said, "I've had more trouble with myself than any other man."

Jesus taught us: *Do not judge others, and you will not be judged. For you will be treated as you treat others. The standard you use in judging is the standard by which you will be judged. And why worry about a speck in your friend's eye when you have a log in your own? How can you think of saying to your friend, 'Let me help you get rid of that speck in your eye,' when you can't see past the log in your own eye? Hypocrite! First get rid of the log in your own eye; then you will see well enough to deal with the speck in your friend's eye. Matthew 7:1-5 NLT*

Yes, this is a word for leaders and for teachers. Human nature is to point our fingers at everyone else. I love the picture in the garden when Adam is confronted by God where God asks, "What happened here?" Then Adam replies, "It was the woman that you gave me." He points in every single other direction. That's human nature. "I'm the victim here. It's everybody else."

Maturity says, "Where am I contributing to the problem?" Maturity seeks feedback and looks for blind spots. I love personal responsibility because it's really powerful.

The ball is in your court; you're not the victim. You have an authority to do something about the situation. I think this is one of the most powerful things I learned in marriage. Kris Vallotton says, "Marriage is a death march to a life camp."

Marriage is the ultimate 'dying to yourself' where you say, "I'm here to serve you. I'm here to love you." This is the maturing process in our walk with God as the bride. It's not about us; it's about dying to self for our groom, the Lord.

It is powerful when you take personal responsibility, because it is something you can change. "God, what do You need to change in me?" Because if it's only the other person's fault, then you are helpless. That's why I love personal responsibility.

Babies are the most selfish individuals on the planet. They're only concerned with their food, their time schedule, and their sleep. That is their world. Then they grow and mature. We teach our kids not to be selfish, to mature, and to start thinking about other people.

We also need to teach ourselves to not be selfish, to be mature, and to grow up in the ways of the Lord.

Questions for reflection:

Has God ever showed you that you need to take your own lenses off and see through His corrective lens? Where has God helped you take personal responsibility where you originally thought the problem was with another person or a group of people?

Around the Table

Lesson 2 Building the House of God

Chris Mathis

We have a responsibility. Our main focus and assignment is to serve and steward the presence of the Lord and minister to people. God has given us a responsibility to this house.

And now for a little while grace has been shown from the LORD our God, to leave us a remnant to escape, and to give us a peg in His holy place, that our God may enlighten our eyes and give us a measure of revival in our bondage. For we were slaves. Yet our God did not forsake us in our bondage; but He extended mercy to us in the sight of the kings of Persia, to revive us, to repair the house of our God, to rebuild its ruins, and to give us a wall in Judah and Jerusalem. Ezra 9:8-9 NKJV

That Scripture is really stunning to me, because this was a time of the Jews' deliverance from captivity. They were rebuilding the temple, rebuilding Jerusalem, and rebuilding the walls. Obviously, that's an Old Testament Scripture, but it has so many spiritual implications for us today in how we build. God in his mercy revived us and called us to build and repair the house of God. We repair its ruins, and He gives us a wall to stand on to intercede on behalf of others in the nation.

Today the church is people, presence, authority, and purpose. Those four points make up the church. I will address three of those here.

1. Let's start with people. Church was always meant to be relational. It's a flock. We're a family. We're a sheep fold. The church *is* people—not programs or a building. The church is 'people' plural, not singular, meaning it doesn't just rally around one man, or one personality, or one leader. It takes the body of Christ in its uniqueness, the people of God, to make it up.

The church is not made up of clergy and laity. Clergy and laity are not terms that we use today in our sector or our denomination. Clergy and laity is predominantly a Catholic term, but we still have a lot of the practices of it in our modern day. In this belief, the clergy are the people who do the work of God, and the laity are the people who come to pay for it; those who watch the clergy. In the Catholic Church, the bishops and priests administer the Word of God. They're the ones who are set apart. There's a line, and everyone else is common. The laity just sit there and support the clergy. That's not God's heart. That's not what the church is.

The church is every gift in the body of Christ working, joining and doing what God has called us all to do. The difference between the past Catholic Church and today is the old Catholic Church would try to keep the body of Christ ignorant in the Word of God.

Moving out of clergy and laity is something that has really impacted me, moving from denominationalism to apostolic families.

Denominationalism is where we must be very careful. As we build, we don't build around this. Denominationalism exists when we rally around a group of people because of a system or set of beliefs that we all agree on. Apostolic families rally around the essential truths, the things we hold with a closed fist, but the trivial things do not have a concrete belief system. We hold them with an open hand.

For example, the Pentecostal Assemblies of God have 16 fundamental truths. When I was a young minister, there was a pastor who was trying to send me to Bible college and the church was going to pay for it. It was an awesome opportunity. I was very humbled that they saw the call of God on my life. The pastor said, "We want to pay for you to be in ministry. You must go down this path." I believed that to a degree, and so I thought, "If I'm going to do what I'm called to do in life, I have to go down this path." And on that path was an Assembly of God Bible College. One of the things that the pastor said was, "Here's the deal, Chris. If you're going to be in the Assemblies of God, you're going to be a Pentecostal preacher. You need to memorize the 16 fundamental truths." So, I got them and studied. I agreed with all of them except for one. I talked about this with him. I asked, "Is this a deal breaker to be a part of this fellowship?" He said, "Yes, if you do not agree, if you do not sign the documentation, that these 16 fundamental truths are not something that you will follow and be a part of, that's unfortunate."

The part I didn't agree with was eschatology. It wasn't even something that really made any difference in the call of God on my life. It was about pre-tribulation theology, which I don't believe in. But that disqualified me from that denomination.

This takes us to apostolic families in an apostolic family. You can sit around a table and one person could be pre-tribulation, another could be post-tribulation, and the last person could be mid-tribulation. Or someone could say we are in the millennial reign of Christ right now. We can have a variety of beliefs.

I think that when we major on minors, we rally around ideas that we believe in, instead of real communion. That common union is Jesus, who is the only One who we should rally around. The thing about eschatologists is every position can prove their point and make you believe it. When you have so many positions, there's something about the mystery of God that we must be okay with and comfortable with and remove this idea that we must have certainty. Everyone should read Ephesians chapter 3; there's mystery that is meant to remain mystery.

Apostolic families give room for mystery and wonder. They give room for creativity, study, and dreaming, and allow people to wonder about the goodness of God and explore the depths. They give room for the riches of Christ without having a dogmatic snake in the ground.

For when one says, "I am of Paul," and another, "I am of Apollos," are you not carnal? Who then is Paul, and who is Apollos, but ministers through whom you believed, as the Lord gave to each one? I planted, Apollos watered, but God gave the increase. So then neither he who plants is anything, nor he who waters, but God who gives the increase. 1 Corinthians 3:4-7 NKJV

In Bible times, that was really a big deal. This is how denominationalism can easily be birthed, even in settings like ours, when in a moment we start crossing those unhealthy lines of, "We're going to do everything this person says. It doesn't matter if I believe it or not." We create divisions and sects based on what we like. We must be careful as we build in this season, to not have different groups that we lean on and receive more from than others. That really causes division instead of union.

Arise, shine; For your light has come! And the glory of the LORD is risen upon you. Isaiah 60:1 NKJV

This is what people should look like: the glory of the Lord. There's a glory on every individual person and we want to pray that glory continues, so we can ultimately know what it truly means to be human and in the likeness of Jesus.

2. It's about presence with lives of prayer. All legitimate Kingdom leadership must be borne by the Spirit and out of presence. I say legitimate leadership because there is a lot of illegitimate leadership in the church, birthed by illegitimate church leaders. Churches that are illegitimate are birthed by wounded leaders, people who served or stepped out before God called them to, because of wounds in their hearts. Ultimately these individuals felt like it was their moment when it really wasn't.

Around the Table

Now the boy Samuel ministered to the Lord before Eli. And the word of the Lord was rare in those days; there was no widespread revelation. And it came to pass at that time, while Eli was lying down in his place, and when his eyes had begun to grow so dim that he could not see, and before the lamp of God went out in the tabernacle of the Lord where the ark of God was, and while Samuel was lying down, that the Lord called Samuel. And he answered, "Here I am!" So he ran to Eli and said, "Here I am, for you called me." And he said, "I did not call; lie down again." And he went and lay down. Then the Lord called yet again, "Samuel!" So Samuel arose and went to Eli, and said, "Here I am, for you called me." He answered, "I did not call, my son; lie down again." (Now Samuel did not yet know the Lord, nor was the word of the Lord yet revealed to him.) And the Lord called Samuel again the third time. So he arose and went to Eli, and said, "Here I am, for you did call me." Then Eli perceived that the Lord had called the boy. Therefore Eli said to Samuel, "Go, lie down; and it shall be, if He calls you, that you must say, 'Speak, Lord, for Your servant hears.'" So Samuel went and lay down in his place. Now the Lord came and stood and called as at other times, "Samuel! Samuel!" And Samuel answered, "Speak, for Your servant hears." 1 Samuel 3:1-10 NKJV

I love that passage of Scripture because of how Samuel related the Father's voice to his spiritual father's voice. There is a time that you hear the Father in your spiritual father, but there comes a point that your spiritual father should train you to hear the voice of the Father that you recognize. In this passage, you can see something in Samuel. Even though he couldn't differentiate the word of the Lord, he was still hungry for the Lord. It says in the very beginning; Eli was in his usual place. It doesn't describe what that place was. It was just a normal place that he had landed in his life that was not where he, a priest, should have been at that season of his life. His usual place should have been before the altar.

Samuel was laying down sleeping in the tabernacle, where the ark of God was. Eli was in his usual place, a place that is not where Samuel was. Eli should have been where Samuel was. But because Samuel was hungry for God, God said, "I'm going to give you presence. I'm going to give you my voice, and I'm going to do a leadership exchange, because you are hungry for the presence of God."

It's evident where people have presence.

3. Lastly, there's authority. The definition of the Kingdom is the rule and reign of God. We talk about the Kingdom, Kingdom people, but many say they have no idea what it means. The Kingdom is the rule and reign of God. It's the dominion of the kings, the King's domain. It's the rule and reign of God and we can have no impact in this life without Kingdom authority on our life. Real Kingdom authority is not just good information. Self-help is important but we need something beyond that. It's something that transcends beyond just good information, education, self-help, how to be a better leader, how to grow, how to study, and how to plan. At the end of the day, all those things do not break yokes or set the captives free from being demon possessed and demonized. Ultimately, I can be a better version of

myself, but I need to be more than a better self; I need to be the best self, with authority and anointing of God on my life.

Behold, I give you the authority to trample on serpents and scorpions, and over all the power of the enemy, and nothing shall by any means hurt you. Luke 10:19 NKJV

The church, especially our charismatic movements, has overemphasized the power of the enemy. Jesus' place does not play into that mindset. He gives us authority over all the power of the enemy. There are different levels in the spirit of darkness. There are ranks in darkness, just like there are ranks and authority in the Kingdom. We have apostolic authority, and prophetic authority; we have people that walk in great deliverance, anointing and authority. What we need to understand is that the greatest revelation of authority comes through us, planted in our hearts and minds knowing that we are blood-bought sons, and nothing with God is impossible, and nothing can harm us.

For David, after he had served his own generation by the will of God, fell asleep, was buried with his fathers, and saw corruption; Acts 13:36 NKJV

That Scripture to me is one of the most beautiful Scriptures in the Bible because it speaks of David's purpose. After he was done with his purpose, he fell asleep and was buried with his fathers. I don't want to stand before the Lord one day and hear him say, "Chris, there was so much more that you should have done and could have done. You just wasted time, and you weren't focused when it was time to be focused." There's a time to play, and there's a time to be focused.

To me, who am less than the least of all the saints, this grace was given, that I should preach among the Gentiles the unsearchable riches of Christ and to make all see what is the fellowship of the mystery, which from the beginning of the ages has been hidden in God who created all things through Jesus Christ. Ephesians 3:8-9 NKJV

The Spirit of the Lord God is upon Me, because the Lord has anointed Me to preach good tidings to the poor; He has sent Me to heal the broken-hearted, to proclaim liberty to the captives. Isaiah 61:1 NKJV

We're a people that need to align properly with the purposes of God. Purpose and alignment go hand in hand. We are called to carry authority that changes cities, atmospheres, nations, states, towns, regions. To do that we have to become who we really are. The enemy has always looked to attack the church. The enemy has its ageless attack, nothing that the enemy ever does is new. It's the same thing since he was called Lucifer in heaven. It's the same thing, because the church is always a representation on earth of the Kingdom of God. This is why church government is so important to me. Proper church government is essential.

Proper government is Kingdom order that brings protection. Remember, there was a war in heaven. That war was over the headship of the Kingdom. Government in the Kingdom always has two things - singular headship and plural leadership. You have the Father, singular headship, but plural leadership through the Son and Holy Spirit. The war in heaven was a governmental war. It was Satan, saying with a third of the angels, "We're going to overthrow the government and do it better". God kicked Satan out. We know this.

What happened next? Another governmental war started but this time it was on the earth. Satan went after Adam. Why? Because he was the head of humankind. Next thing you know, Satan went after Jesus because He was the first fruit of redemption. He was the head. He was the One who brought in new creation. Satan tried to go to war with Jesus. It was a governmental issue. When it was taken a step further, Satan went to war with Peter, the head of the church. Jesus went to Peter and said, "Satan has asked to sift you like wheat, but I prayed for you." It's the same attack over and over, and Satan's doing it in churches. He's doing it in families. He's trying to do it in fathers, and in homes.

The family is so important with good headship at home. This is why preaching on manhood is so important today. There's an attack on manhood with the feminist agenda. The war has always been the same. It's after headship.

This is where that Absalom spirit comes in. The Absalom spirit really identifies himself under a cloak of 'doing right' but really looks more like Satan than anything. This is the ageless attack on repeat. He plays the same hand of cards every single time.

We see it in the story of Absalom. He had a sister, Tamar. They had a half-brother named Amnon, all sons and daughters of David. One day, Amnon looked at Tamar and said, "This woman is beautiful. I want to be with her." So, he pretended to be sick to get her to take care of him. It was a manipulative move, and he ended up raping his sister.

After Amnon raped Tamar, she was confused, and he kicked her to the curb. She felt even more shame and ran to her brother, Absalom, with whom she lived for a time.

David was informed of everything that went on. Unfortunately, he didn't do anything about this situation, which Absalom thought was wrong because he believed what happened to his sister was not right. And as he looked to the headship, who said he would do nothing, a wedge of bitterness born out of a good intention formed in Absalom. Absalom decided to take matters into his own hands, and he killed his stepbrother, Amnon. He began getting applause from people because of it. Then Absalom tried to take headship of the king. It was a dysfunctional Kingdom order, an ageless attack.

The Kingdom has proper alignment, and we all have a part to play in that, but it's for protection. This is a season to build the house of God. People, presence, and authority are what make up the Kingdom; they are what make up the house of God.

Question for reflection:

What does it look like in your present season to build the house of God?

Around the Table

Lesson 3 Team Growth

Heather Paton

Teams are an integral part of churches, and it is important to help your team grow. There are three stages of team growth that were shared with me as a young leader by Pastor Jay Haizlip.

1. First is the *family stage*. In the family stage, all hands are required on deck. When we planted the Summit West campus location, it was about, "Who's here, who has a heartbeat, who can function, and what can they do?"

The family stage is like a social group made up of parents and children. You work with what you have. They can do the job; they may not do it well or be a pro, but they can help get the job done. They're excited to serve and be a part of the family. They're surprised and maybe shaken by problems that come.

Let's use 'Uncle Pete' as an example. When you plant a church, Uncle Pete is the type of guy that shows up to the barbecue; he may not be great on the grill, it's quite possible he will burn every hot dog, but you're ok with that. You're just thankful that Uncle Pete is manning the barbecue because you don't have the capacity to cook hotdogs alongside all of the other things you're leading. People like Uncle Pete are usually just thrilled to be a part of the team. They are usually teachable, and you can help them improve their skills.

Sometimes in leadership, you may be surrounded by more passion than skill but be thankful for the 'Uncle

Pete's who are ready to serve the vision whether skilled or not. They might not have a lot of talent and gifting, but they've got passion.

2. The next stage would be the *capability stage*. This is the power or ability to do something. In other words, people do what needs to be done. Oftentimes, others don't see what needs to be done, but they'll do what you've asked them to do. They deal with problems as they come, even if they don't see them coming, because they'll have some sort of capability to deal with them (or at least know your heart in dealing with problems). You're starting to get them to the honey spot. These are growing leaders.

3. The next stage to team growth would be *special operations*, a pursuit or area of study or skill to which someone has devoted much time and effort, in which they're an expert.

Compare Uncle Pete to a chef. When the chef arrives, he's going to add some spices and flavours that will enhance the experience. He knows how to grill to perfection. He knows what people like, and he can deliver every time. These are the special operations people. They're highly competent. They don't wait to be told what to do. They know what needs to be done even before they're asked to do it. They foresee problems. These are people who think ahead saying, "If we're going to make this decision, then we have to be ready for some pushback here, or if we're going to make that decision, this is likely what will happen...." They can see a step ahead.

As leaders, we're going to continually be working with people at all different stages. It's important for us to know what stage people are at because if we have someone at a family stage and we're looking for them to be at a special operations stage, we're going to become very frustrated with them. On the flipside, if we have someone who's a special operations type, and we're giving them family stage responsibility, they're going to feel underused, and they might walk away because they have so much more to give. It's knowing who you can pour into, and how much responsibility you can give to people, and being able to navigate both.

As your team grows or as other people are coming in, there will be some who are like Uncle Pete, burning hot dogs every week, and a skilled special operations person like 'Phil' might come in to replace them. Uncle Pete may lack maturity in recognizing Phil's gift because he fears being replaced. We need to teach Uncle Pete to say, "Phil, you do this a lot better than me. I'm willing to learn, but this is actually your gifting." There's a difference between being replaced and being repositioned.

That is not a demotion but a promotional key to growing a team. We want people growing. In these opportunities we can hand off the tongs or fight to hold onto the tongs, being less than the best.

It's a 'trust the process' moment with the Lord and being able to say, "Do I really trust that the Lord has the best interests for me? Do I really believe that anyone can take me out of the will of God?"

Around the Table

There's such value in a team and looking around the table. There's many of us who ran alone for so long, and being part of a team is so rewarding. It's rewarding to sit around the table with people who are at all different stages and to recognize, "Hey this person is really great at this job. I could do it. I'm capable of doing it, but they're incredible at doing it," and be able to release that job to them.

Let's not hold onto any job or role too tightly. There are certain people who might have an outreach gift or an administration gift, but they might do it differently. One isn't better than the other because the outcome will be the same. Sometimes it might just be best for you not to watch how they're doing it.

We had a girl on our team who did things differently than me. We would always get to the same point, but her process stressed me out, so I would walk away. She would always execute it, but her process and her logical thinking was completely contrary to my creative way of thinking. Neither was right or better, just different.

A good leader or coach will see your potential and call it out. You can be trained with the skills and talents that you need to be able to get to where you want to be. You might not have them now but that doesn't mean you're never going to have them.

At some point we're going to fail the people we lead. It's never intentional, it just happens. Someone might come to you and say, "You really hurt my feelings when this happened." You can accidentally hurt someone's heart and fail them as their leader by not noticing something important or accidentally disregarding them.

We need to help those we lead be dependent on Christ and rooted in Him. That way, if there's a situation, and we're not there, they know what to do. They can think on their own.

God's word is alive and powerful. A good leader will make sure to impart a desire to serve the people. We need to sit at His feet, not just at our leadership table. So many people want to sit at our team's table when they need to be sitting at His feet first. Both are vital, but one is primary. We want to impart that they need to be sitting at His feet first.

As team leaders, modeling serving from a position of rest is important. Man plans his way; the Lord directs his steps.

We live in a culture of striving. For people that we mentor or disciple, we need to let them know that nothing is going to get them where they need to be sooner than the Lord's timing. We've all probably been somewhere before the Lord's timing because of our striving, and it's caused some friction in our walk. It's caused some agitation, disappointment, and lots of frustration. Model serving from a position of rest, knowing that the Lord will get them exactly where He needs them to be in His time.

As leaders, we need to celebrate tour team member's growth. Remembering where people started is important because sometimes, we can get frustrated with people and think, "How do they not know yet?" Realize that while some people might have 10, 15, 20 years of ministry experience, others will have two years or less. Let go of expectations and celebrate where people are at, even if it's a little growth.

As team leaders, we must recognize which stage people are at. If someone is at the family stage, and you're expecting a special operations stage, you will be frustrated. If we expect that level of performance, we will break the person who is at the family stage. They'll feel overwhelmed and feel like they can never measure up.

We need to be gracious with them. We will be receiving people at all the different stages and it's important for us as leaders to ask for wisdom from the Lord on where to place them, how to grow them, how to challenge them, and how to humble them. We need wisdom as leaders.

We want them to feel skilled, encouraged, and empowered. People desire to grow. If you study David when he brought in the disgruntled men, the discontented men, they were the rejects of society. Later, you see all the things that they conquered and all the things that they did. It's awesome to see how he worked with them where they were at; whatever stage they came in, he just worked with them.

We've been given people at all the different stages, and we just want to empower them to be able to grow to get to the special operations level and not damage them in the process.

Leadership Lessons from The Summit

Questions for reflection:

How well do you grow someone from a family stage to a special operations stage? What stage is your team at right now?

Around the Table

Lesson 4 The Cost of Discipleship

Chris Mathis

There's a cost to discipleship. Salvation is free, but discipleship costs our whole lives. It is not about a one-time decision, but about decision after decision to lay down our motives and ambitions.

As massive crowds followed Jesus, he turned to them and said, "When you follow me as my disciple, you must put aside your father, your mother, your wife, your sisters, your brothers; it will even seem as though you hate your own life. This is the price you'll pay to be considered one of my followers. Anyone who comes to me must be willing to share my cross and experience it as his own, or he cannot be considered to be my disciple. So don't follow me without considering what it will cost you. For who would construct a house before first sitting down to estimate the cost to complete it? Otherwise, he may lay the foundation and not be able to finish. The neighbors will ridicule him, saying, 'Look at him! He started to build but couldn't complete it!' "Have you ever heard of a commander who goes out to war without first sitting down with strategic planning to determine the strength of his army to win the war against a stronger opponent? If he knows he doesn't stand a chance of winning the war, the wise commander will send out delegates to ask for the terms of peace. Likewise, unless you surrender all to me, giving up all you possess, you cannot be one of my disciples. Luke 14:25-33 TPT

There are two verses I want to highlight: verse 26 and verse 33. Verse 26 says, *"You must put aside your father, your mother, your wife, your sisters, your brothers, yes. You will even seem as though you hate your own life."* Then later, verse 33 says, *"Likewise, unless you surrender, ultimately giving up all you possess, you cannot be one of my disciples."*

How many of you have ever heard these verses and thought, "Man, I would never measure up."?

I used to preach that if you don't do what these Scriptures say, you're basically a pathetic Christian. In a lot of ways, that was the kind of mindset and teaching I was under, and I was pretending I was living these values out in my own life. I was projecting I was doing that, but I was just like everyone else, still struggling on the inside with these verses.

However, I want to put a different spin on these verses because as I reread these verses and review notes of mine from almost a decade ago, I see it through a new lens. When reading these verses, often we think about natural possessions, money, houses, cars, etc.; if you're not willing to give it all up, you can't be a disciple of Jesus, right?

Many Christians even try to apply the part about being willing to put aside their family and use the Scripture as an excuse to be a jerk to their own family members. But that's not really what Jesus is saying. He's not saying to cut off your family. Instead, there's something deeper here. I think we've misinterpreted these Scriptures and applied them in the natural when in reality they have more to do with the spiritual and the soul than they do natural possessions.

When Jesus was saying to put aside your father and mother, He was not contradicting the Scripture where it talks about honouring your father and mother. What if He was saying He's untethering you from the cultural upbringing that you were in? What if He's saying that unless you can lay down who you are—your race, your ethnicity, your cultural upbringing, everything that you hold so close and dear to your heart—you can't be one of His?

We read these passages many times and we often think it's about natural possessions, money, homes, or the things that we own, but what if the Scripture really refers to the internal part of you?

I've watched lives condemned when reading these passages, and people not feeling like they can ever measure up because of the tension.

Instead, I want to submit that what Jesus was actually talking about was the soul and spirit.

What if He wasn't talking about your money, but rather your fears? What if He wasn't talking about your possessions, but rather your ambitions? Let's take it a step further.

What if He wasn't talking about letting go of things that you hold in your hand? What if He was talking about things that you hold dear to your heart, like your accomplishments, your demand for respect, your need for control, or your need for applause and approval? Unless you surrender all to Him and give it up? What if it's not about what I possess but all that's in my heart, all that I have thought, and how I am wired?

I wanted to bring these different perspectives of the Scriptures so that you don't have to live condemned. If you're feeling condemned, you don't have to live your life feeling guilty because you read that passage and you think, "Well, I just never measure up. I can barely live, and I want to do more, but I feel like I can't because I have natural things in my life."

Paul said, "If you don't take care of your house, you're worse than an infidel." (1 Tim 5:8 paraphrased) So, there's responsibility on our part to have possessions to be able to provide. I don't think Jesus is talking about possessions in Luke 14:25-33; I believe He's talking about something deeper.

If this is the case, who would you be? Some of the questions I asked myself were, "Who would I be without fear? What would my life look like if it had no fear?"

Who would you be without ambition? Who would you be without your accomplishments, your degrees, or successes identifying you? Who would you be if no one respected you? Who would you be if you had no need to control everything? Who would you be if you didn't get a thumbs up or an applause from everyone?

To be clear, we all need affirmation. But I think what the Lord wants to do in us is not live by the praise of man and the affirmation of people. The affirmation comes from Him. When we are able to fully surrender all of those things in ourselves—our fears, our ambitions, our accomplishments, our need for respect, our need for a title, our need for position, our need to be identified as something in someone else's eyes— it's great.

Jesus says unless you can lay it all down, you cannot be His disciple. In life, we're going through a process of discipleship, every one of us, where there are things God is chiseling away in our internal world. There are things that we must lay down and say, "You know what? I still have elements of fear in my life. There are decisions I sometimes make out of fear not faith. Fear, not love. There are decisions I make because I need to control a situation instead of trusting God."

But rather than staying here, what if we take this acknowledgement a step further and say, "You can have this, Lord. It is yours."? What if we were willing to lay down our lives, heart and soul, with all our motives and ambitions so that we could be the disciples He created us to be?

Questions for reflection:

How did you look at these two Scriptures from Luke before? How do they impact you in a way that might be negative? What is it that is hard for you to let go of, to surrender to the Lord?

Around the Table

Lesson 5 The Wine is Worth the Wait

Paulina Guinez

I'm not a wine expert, but the Lord likes to show me what He is doing through pictures and photos so I can relate and understand Him and myself better.

An interesting fact about wine is that making wine naturally is a long, slow process. It can take up to three years to get from the initial planting to the actual harvest and crushing. Additionally, from those three years, it could take, depending on the aging, years before it even enters a bottle. Interestingly, different environments produce different flavor profiles. Poorly pruned vines simply won't produce high-quality fruit, and ultimately, it is with high-quality fruit that winemakers can make high-quality wine.

The differences between cheap wine and expensive wine interested me. Cheap wine is easy to drink as it has a large quantity of low-quality grapes, whereas expensive wine is hand-picked and is aged for several years; in expensive wine, there is a smaller amount of grapes, yet they are higher quality. Additionally, cheap wine is not a natural process as it contains additives to make up for the lower quality of grapes. It is more chemical based with added sugars for sweetness. Instead of waiting for the wine to process and smooth, sugars and stabilizers are added to cheap wine during the production. Cheaper wine is manipulated more by man and machine to save money and time. Rather than using authentic barrels, chips and staves are added to the wine to produce a "natural" taste of oakiness, therefore creating a non-authentic process. In contrast, expensive wine uses natural flavor profiles, has no additives, and is matured for years in oak barrels with natural flavors.

The bulk of cheap wines are made from grapes grown in hot regions with fertile soil, which grows crops easily, but lacks complexity. It is super simple and mainstream. However, with expensive wines, the best vines grow where there is a struggle such as on hills with low nutrient soil or near rivers providing fertile ground.

This makes me ponder how things in life can be perceived as "fertile soil" (things that grow and produce quickly), making people believe that this must be the most successful way to live, produce, and succeed. I wonder how many people will brave a more expensive process.

Expensive wines have increased levels of tannins, giving the wine a more complex profile. Tannins are molecules that help give wine structure and mature flavor by making it richer, smoother, and less harsh. In the beginning stages of wine, tannins are super bitter, but through the process of time, the tannins help deepen and mature the wine's flavor profile. Expensive wine takes time to smooth out, become more complex, and provide deeper flavors.

In cheap wines, winemakers produce the wine right away while it is super bitter, hiding the taste with sweeteners.

Cheap wine is meant to be consumed quickly and have a short shelf life; it is not designed for aging. A fresh bottle of cheap wine will have a bright fruity taste, which disappears with age as flavors fade and the wine becomes dull. Expensive wine has no worry of spoilage, and it has complex flavors that come out with age; it is always worth the wait.

Cheap wine has a surface-level taste—you're going to taste whatever the strongest flavor is—whereas with expensive wine, there's a deeper level taste that you would not have noticed in the beginning that comes to the surface in time.

Cheap wine is not set up for the future; it is for the now. Expensive wine is set up for the future; it ages well.

I just love these pictures, and I believe that the Lord likes to put beautiful things around us, like vineyards, so that we can see beauty in the process: the beauty, the waiting, and the reward of aging and yielding. The type of vessel we are in and the amount of process time matters. The more time we are in process, the more that gets pulled out of us—ultimately smoothing and refining us to become who God originally intended us to be. Each day, month, and year means more richness, stability, smoothing of our edges, maturing, and yielding to the process of the Winemaker and the way He wants us to be flavored. He desires for us to be poured out and have all the necessary flavors, tones, and richness, not masks, cover ups, short shelf lives, surface tones, and flavors.

As I was researching wine, the Lord gave me a picture of Himself opening an old wine cellar and grabbing and popping open aged wines that were ready to be poured out over the earth. I believe He has already started pouring out His new wine into our new wineskin, and the more we let Him age and flavour us, the more that we can mature and stand the test of time. While the other cheaper and less expensive wines fade, lose texture, taste, and spoil, I want to be a wine that pours out for the rest of my life and does not lose flavor; I want to be a wine that only gets more rich, purer, and more complex.

Questions for reflection:

Have you ever rushed or wanted to rush through the processes of the Lord quickly? Does your life hold the flavors of a cheap or expensive wine? What is preventing you from a deeper process?

Lesson 6 Deliverance

Tracy Belford

The first time I saw a deliverance I was about 20. I watched in awe and afterwards asked the people doing it how they did it. They explained the basics of deliverance. The next morning, someone manifested demonically in front of me. Jesus told me, "It's your turn now." So, I cast that demon out, with literally 20 minutes of teaching in me. I marvelled afterward about it, but the truth is, the disciples weren't even saved yet when Jesus sent them out to heal and deliver people. They just did it in His name, and that was enough.

The seventy-two returned with joy and said, "Lord, even the demons submit to us in your name." He replied, "I saw Satan fall like lightning from heaven. I have given you authority to trample on snakes and scorpions and to overcome all the power of the enemy; nothing will harm you. However, do not rejoice that the spirits submit to you, but rejoice that your names are written in heaven. Luke 10:17-20 NIV

We don't need anything to be able to do deliverance in the name of Jesus; however, training can help. After all, the disciples had watched Jesus do deliverance before they went out and did it.

In most services we have at Summit, people get delivered. Sometimes it is simply through self-deliverance, where the person is worshipping, and they come out of lies they have believed and embrace the truth about what God says. Other times it is clearly a deliverance session where one person is helping another get free. Either way, deliverance is happening all the time.

In our deliverance team, we do deliverance sessions weekly. We have a long waitlist of people who want to get free. What we do there is different than what happens on a Sunday. When the person comes, they have filled out a package about their entire life, which allows us to find the roots of what is going on, rather than just dealing with whatever the problem of the moment is. But can you imagine if our entire church was actually equipped to cast out demons? It would be so much easier. There would be no waitlist, there would just be freedom.

Every month I get people coming to me asking me to teach them how to do deliverance. Our body wants to know what to do and how to be empowered. The Bible says,

He said to them, "Go into all the world and preach the gospel to all creation. Whoever believes and is baptized will be saved, but whoever does not believe will be condemned. And these signs will accompany those who believe: In my name they will drive out demons; they will speak in new tongues; they will pick up snakes with their hands; and when they drink deadly poison, it will not hurt them at all; they will place their hands on sick people, and they will get well." Mark 16:15-18 NIV

In this Scripture, driving out demons is equated with speaking in tongues, being healed of poison, and healing people. Have you ever considered that casting out a demon is as easy as speaking in tongues?

I've outlined the very basics of deliverance so that you can go and teach others.

Possession and oppression happen because of an agreement with a lie. The truth sets them free. Usually, deliverance is as easy as:

1. Identify the lie.

2. Renounce the lie and repent of partnering with it.

3. Accept the truth.

For example, I renounce the lie that I am unloved, and I accept the truth that Jesus loves me. Someone says that, and the next thing you know, they are experiencing freedom like they have never known. Sometimes deliverance comes with manifestations and shrieking, and sometimes it does not.

There are four main doors to oppression: fear, witchcraft, sexual sin, and trauma. If someone opens a door to these things and allows sin a foothold, they begin experiencing oppression. Also, in some people, the sins of the generations before them hold them in oppression, such as freemasonry, or occult practices and idolatry in their family line.

The two most common issues I see in every person who comes to us for deliverance are rejection and abandonment. If you don't know where to start, these are a good starting point.

How do you know if someone is struggling with possession or oppression? Look in their eyes. You can see it. You can also often see it in their facial expressions if you are looking closely enough. But if you can't tell, you can always ask them questions, like, "What are you feeling right now?" Ask them if it's a good feeling or a bad feeling. If they can identify, for example, that they feel afraid, then you can continue to ask them what they are afraid of, or when they started feeling afraid. Once you get to the memory, you start getting them to ask Jesus questions, which leads them to truth and revelation from Jesus.

I want to tell you the story of a girl who came to church a while ago. She was overtly manifesting in the foyer at True North. It was 30 degrees below zero that day, and she would run outside with no coat, run around the parking lot, then come back in, speaking in demon tongues, shrieking and writhing. Someone called for me to come and I did, but there were already a few people praying with her. Because she was making a scene, I took her into a different room.

Demons are attention seeking, and a lot of their manifestations are simply to take attention off Jesus and onto themselves. When we were in the room, the other people were in there trying to yell at the demon to come out. That rarely works. They aren't cast out by our volume, but rather because of the authority of Jesus we carry. Understanding that the power that raised Christ from the dead lives in you is important to the process, because if you don't believe it, then you have no authority. I settled her down, and asked her some questions, but the demon only wanted to lie and not tell me anything of value. Anything I asked the girl to repent of, she would not.

After a while, I decided it was not worth wasting my time on someone who did not want to be free. I walked away. I watched her for the rest of the service so that she was not going to make a spectacle. Then, when the altar call came, I watched her walk down to the front, ready to repent. I went down and joined her, and because she was ready and wanted to repent, it came out with no fuss, no noise, and no more manifestations.

I get frustrated sometimes because I want demons to leave the way they did for Jesus. Easier. With less effort. To command them and they leave immediately. And sometimes it does happen that way. But I continue to pray that it would be that way more often. Jesus told his disciples that it was about faith.

"Lord, have mercy on my son," he said. "He has seizures and is suffering greatly. He often falls into the fire or into the water. I brought him to your disciples, but they could not heal him." "You unbelieving and perverse generation," Jesus replied, "how long shall I stay with you? How long shall I put up with you? Bring the boy here to me." Jesus rebuked the demon, and it came out of the boy, and he was healed at that moment. Then the disciples came to Jesus in private and asked, "Why couldn't we drive it out?" He replied, "Because you have so little faith. Truly I tell you, if you have faith as small as a mustard seed, you can say to this mountain, 'Move from here to there,' and it will move. Nothing will be impossible for you." Matthew 17:15-20 NIV

If you want to be able to walk in the calling of deliverance, ask for more faith, because it is a key to deliverance. I also believe deliverance gives us more faith. I could never walk away from Jesus after seeing what I have seen. When you see a demon tormenting someone, and then see that person get free, the world loses its appeal. The cost of watching demonic movies just isn't worth it to me. The reality of the unseen world sets in when you see someone be delivered.

Ultimately, you have the ability to deliver people. When you sense a demon, command it to leave in Jesus' name. If it doesn't leave right away, ask some questions. Try to figure out what the lie was. Renounce it. Repent. Accept the truth. Then command the demon to leave in the name of Jesus. Listen to what Jesus tells you because there is no formula. Jesus has the answers every time, and everything we do needs to be done in relationship with Him.

Questions for reflection:

Because it is a part of our commission as Christians, do you feel confident that you can deliver someone and/or teach others how? How can we as a church empower our body to fulfil this part of our commission?

Lesson 7 Creativity

Heather Paton

There are many types of creativity. From artsy people to compartmentalized to analytical to logical, we're all created in the likeness of the Lord, which means we all carry some sort of creativity.

God has always moved creatively in and through objects to people. We see that for Moses in the tabernacle, and through Noah and the ark. He was highly creative, building a simple wooden boat, yet in the hands of God, it became a prophetic symbol and a vehicle of redemption and promise to generations to come. David was a psalmist, who laid in the pastures with his smelly sheep and wrote songs, declarations, and poems to the Lord. We still sing many of those today. But he also had the ability to sing and worship and cast out tormenting spirits from the pureness of his worship.

Most artists can deal with various challenges in their creative lives, but comparison can be very real for people in this culture. We have highly anointed, talented people, such as worship leaders, instrumentalists, writers, etc., but for some, it takes a lot of energy and courage to jump into those things when they're new, young, or unsure of themselves, or second guessing the calling on their life.

It's important for us, no matter what aspect of creativity that we're in, to always have someone to ask, "Hey, you're a couple of steps ahead of me—can you share with me? How do I grow? How do I challenge myself? I don't want to be like you, but I want to grow in different areas that I need to grow in."

The more we do this, the more trustworthy we become. If we don't yield to the process of growing, we'll never get better. We need to decide we want to be a better guitar player, singer, builder, or basketball player, for example, however, if we never allow ourselves to be diligent, to be trustworthy in the things that the Lord has called us to, then we will never actually grow in those gifts.

When it seems like someone else might surpass us, we don't want to do it. But beauty and creating isn't about being the best. It's about doing what we know we're created to do. And I think when we yield to that process, it makes creativity very light. It makes that process easy.

I hosted a writer's retreat, and I was surrounded by a bunch of writers. There's some who shared their work, and I said, "Wow, my brain doesn't even think on a wavelength like that." But that's okay because my brain doesn't function like that. There's beauty, and I don't need to function in comparison, but instead, enjoy the beauty in what other people are releasing.

We must master techniques, processes, and ways of doing things in life, and practice and function in them to make them all work together in harmony. For many artists, this is an ongoing process of looking for more inspiring subject matters. And it's really a connection with the Lord on how to release the new things. What we create by living in the Kingdom is a representation of what God wants to do around the earth.

I was talking with Tracy about writing a book, and I said to her that it seemed silly for me to write a book because there are other people that have written books on similar topics, so who would want to read another one? She said, "Me, because I read one book and then I want to read another one and another one and another one."

Then I realized, "Oh, people do that." There are a lot of people who just love to consume. They love to read so much. However, if a writer says, 'There's something I feel I am to write, but somebody else has already written something similar. The writer begins to think there is no purpose. But that is wrong thinking.

In the past, Jamie preached a message at our old church. We had a visiting minister who came in and preached the same message the following week, and our congregation said, "Wow, this was life changing!" If you were to listen to both messages, they were so similar—about 80% of the content was the same—but what was released by the visiting minister awoke people in a different way.

It doesn't matter if people get the message from me, but just that they actually get it. If they get freedom from reading a book on deliverance that someone else wrote, and not from my book, then it doesn't matter, as long as they get the revelation of the main message.

About eight years ago, a lady in London, Ontario, called me and said that she was starting a ministry. It was called *Women in Ministry*. It was a national ministry. And she said she wanted me to champion the southwestern Ontario region. I thought it was cool, but I didn't do music, and I didn't do media, so I wasn't super qualified, but I did it anyway.

Now, years later it makes sense that God was preparing me even though I felt it wasn't my lane. Sometimes God is preparing us for something coming down the road that we cannot yet see. And ultimately, our obedience to the process is what is important.

Questions for reflection:

Are there any areas that God is calling you to press into and practice your skill? In what way do you see that Yahweh is asking you to create with Him in this season?

Lesson 8 Old Testament vs New Testament

Chris Frost

Growing up and reading the Bible, it seemed to me that the God of the Old Testament was very different from the God of the New Testament. However, what I've begun to realize is that God wasn't different, and he didn't change. It was my understanding of Him that needed to change.

I started to dive into Exodus 34:6-7. This is the first time in the Bible where God revealed His character. In this section of Scripture, God had revealed himself to Israel and told them that he wanted to be in covenant relationship with them. They agreed and so Moses went up the mountain to receive the details of what this covenant was going to look like, namely, the 10 commandments. Moses took a long time (40 days) on the mountain and while he was up there, the Israelites made the golden calf. Then Moses came down the mountain, smashed the tablets, then went back up the mountain, and had an encounter with God. Moses was interceding for the people so that God wouldn't leave them or destroy them. Moses asked God to show him His glory, or in other words, asked God, "Show me what You're really like." And this is what He said:

The Lord passed before him and proclaimed, "The Lord, the Lord, a God merciful and gracious, slow to anger, and abounding in steadfast love and faithfulness, keeping steadfast love for thousands, forgiving iniquity and transgression and sin, but who will by no means clear the guilty, visiting the iniquity of the fathers on the children and the children's children, to the third and the fourth generation." Exodus 34:6-7 ESV

As I was studying this, I thought, "It starts out really good. But that last part sounds a little vindictive. That's the God of the Old Testament. The punishment is going to come."

Where was my understanding wrong? Because if God is good all the time, how am I understanding it wrong?

I came to realize Israel didn't have a relationship with God. They didn't really know Him yet. They knew Him as their Deliverer; however, they were experienced with other gods. Their belief was, "If we sacrifice, maybe, just maybe we'll find favor, but maybe we won't. Maybe this will happen. Maybe it won't."

What God was communicating in this Scripture was: "I'm going to be consistent. I'm going to be unchanging." That's a big deal. He was revealing His tendency to be merciful, to be loving, to forgive sin.

But if people don't want to be forgiven, if they don't want to be cleared from their sin, then they experience the consequences of that.

We have this idea of punishment, of plagues, of all these things coming down on the people, but most often, punishment in the Bible is people experiencing the consequences of their sin.

So, what does it mean when I get punished for my sin? Does it mean I get punished for my father and grandfather's sin? Well, no, but if this is how I was raised, and I continue to live in it and not change from it, then I'm going to experience the consequences of all those things.

So, is God angry with me? No, because He has a tendency—no, a default—to forgive. Interestingly, this verse, Exodus 34:6-7, is the most quoted verse in the Old Testament, by other prophets and people. It's most often quoted when someone is interceding for forgiveness on behalf of a nation, and they appeal to God's mercy.

One example that I love is Jonah in Nineveh, when Jonah didn't want to go because of how bad the Assyrians were. If you had a people like that, who were oppressing you, what would you want to happen to them? You would probably want them to be punished, right? Jonah went and spoke to them. They repented, and then Jonah complained to God, *"Oh, Lord, is this not what I said? When I was still at home? That is why I was so quick to flee to Tarshish. I knew that You are a gracious and compassionate God, slow to anger and abounding in love. God, I knew You were like this. I knew You were compassionate. And I didn't want to go because I wanted them punished. And I knew if I went, You were going to be compassionate to them."* Jonah 4-2-3 NIV

This is who God is. John describes Jesus as the same as the God revealed in the Old Testament.

And the Word became flesh and dwelt among us, and we have seen his glory, glory as of the only Son from the Father, full of grace and truth. John 1:14 ESV

In the Septuagint, which is a Greek writing of the Old Testament, it refers to these verses. John was saying, "Jesus is the same man as God was back then." Jesus revealed Himself as the same man that revealed Himself to Moses in the rock. John didn't see a difference between the Old Testament and the New Testament.

God from the Old Testament, and God from the New Testament, are the same. They're the same person. This is revealing of who God is, and what His character is.

The word iniquity in Hebrew is *"Avon"*. But it means crooked. If we lay out a crooked path for someone to follow, that's the path that they're going to probably follow.

What does the phrase, "They have to learn something the hard way" mean? Well, it usually means carrying the weight of your sin; that you must suffer the consequences. We inherently know that this is punishment for our sin.

As Christians, we often feel like we must continue to bear the burden first. I talk with lots of people in my office who need to understand this. We do an exercise where we give stuff over to Jesus because we feel like we know that we were wrong. We need to bear the burden of the sin before we feel sorry.

We know in our heads that Jesus forgives us, but we don't experience that forgiveness because we feel like we must carry the weight of it; that somehow in carrying the weight of it and experiencing the consequences of it, we will be changed.

We do what Adam and Eve did. We hide our sin and then in hiding it, we don't allow forgiveness to come. But the picture the Bible gives is that Jesus took this *Avon* upon Himself and allowed it to crush Him.

But he was pierced for our transgressions; he was crushed for our iniquities; upon him was the chastisement that brought us peace, and with his wounds we are healed. Isaiah 53:5 ESV

He was without sin and allowed our sins to crush Him so that we no longer needed to be crushed by it. So, what do we need to do to be free from this? Just confess; tell Jesus, "Hey, I'm letting this thing crush me. I'm going to give it to You."

We try to solve the problem of our own sin, but we can't, which is why Jesus solved it for us.

If we confess our sins, he is faithful and just to forgive us our sins and to cleanse us from all unrighteousness. 1 John 1:9 ESV

And it gives us this picture in Psalm 32:

Blessed is the one whose transgression is forgiven, whose sin is covered. Blessed is the man against whom the Lord counts no iniquity, and in whose spirit there is no deceit. For when I kept silent, my bones wasted away through my groaning all day long. For day and night your hand was heavy upon me; my strength was dried up as by the heat of summer. I acknowledged my sin to you, and I did not cover my iniquity; I said, "I will confess my transgressions to the Lord," and you forgave the iniquity of my sin.

Around the Table

Therefore, let everyone who is godly offer prayer to you at a time when you may be found; surely in the rush of great waters, they shall not reach him. You are a hiding place for me; you preserve me from trouble; you surround me with shouts of deliverance. I will instruct you and teach you in the way you should go; I will counsel you with my eye upon you. Be not like a horse or a mule, without understanding, which must be curbed with bit and bridle, or it will not stay near you. Many are the sorrows of the wicked, but steadfast love surrounds the one who trusts in the Lord. Be glad in the Lord, and rejoice, O righteous, and shout for joy, all you upright in heart! Psalm 32:1-11 ESV

Questions for reflection:

Father, where have I misunderstood You in Scripture? Are there places where I believe something about Your character that isn't true? Is there anything that I am punishing myself for that You have already solved on the cross?

Lesson 9 Managing Our Inner Man

Chris Mathis

As leaders, we deal with situations where people are constantly on a treadmill of trying to become the word they're looking for. Managing our private world or inner man is important.

We are platform oriented; that is, we like getting glory from the praise of man or putting our identity in what we do for God instead of being a son or a daughter of God and just being content with being loved.

This really comes down to an internal inner world issue. Your inner man is your soul, which is your mind, your will, and your emotions.

Did you know we need self-care? The soul gets wounded. The soul gets its feelings hurt. The soul gets confused. If you're soul-led and not Spirit-led, you're not going to perceive truth properly.

As leaders, it's very easy to see this trend in North American culture. There's a pressure to have it all together on the outside 100% of the time in front of everyone. There's this constant pressure placed on us by society. We're trained that way from little children all the way into adulthood.

As a result, we learn how to suppress our inner world, our soul, when it could be in turmoil. It can be in shambles, and we learn to become professional fakers.

For example, we've been taught in our culture that busyness is success. If I asked you, "Hey, how's your week going? What's been going on in your world lately?" The typical North American response is, "It's been awesome, but busy." We won't often say to someone, "It's been awesome. But I haven't done anything. It's been awesome, but I was just sitting around." That's typically not what we say when we're projecting an image to someone. We equate busyness with success. Tasks with success. Goals with success. We want to project an image that even when it's not busy, we say it's busy.

To understand better, let's compare Saul and John the Baptist.

First, Saul was a called man. We see this in Scripture—he was called and ordained of God.

Then the Spirit of the Lord will come upon you, and you will prophesy with them and be turned into another man. 1 Samuel 10:6 NKJV

Samuel anointed Saul as he was looking for his father's donkeys. Saul was a called man. Calling and anointing were on his life.

Second, we see that Saul lived in great insecurity. He was an insecure leader. Insecure leaders create insecure leaders. They have to use control and manipulation. We see this all throughout Saul's life.

In 1 Samuel 10:21-23, we see Saul hiding from people at his inauguration. He's hiding, not in humility, but in insecurity. It appears he's being humble, but his hiding is rooted in pride. He's hiding because he doesn't see himself the way God sees him. It looks like humility, but it is insecurity.

Lastly, we see that Saul lived in great fear.

So David went out wherever Saul sent him, and behaved wisely. And Saul set him over the men of war, and he was accepted in the sight of all the people and also in the sight of Saul's servants. Now it had happened as they were coming home, when David was returning from the slaughter of the Philistine, that the women had come out of all the cities of Israel, singing and dancing, to meet King Saul, with tambourines, with joy, and with musical instruments. So the women sang as they danced, and said: "Saul has slain his thousands, And David his ten thousands." Then Saul was very angry, and the saying displeased him; and he said, "They have ascribed to David ten thousands, and to me they have ascribed only thousands. Now what more can he have but the kingdom?" So Saul eyed David from that day forward.
1 Samuel 18:5-9 NKJV

There were women singing with tambourines, and the number one hit on the charts in Israel that day was '*Saul killed the thousands and David killed the tens of thousands*'. This was erupting through their culture. Saul heard this trendy song everywhere. As a leader, his heart should have said, "That's awesome. This is a young one that's coming after me. He's doing what I could not do on my own." But instead, Saul lived in great fear that David was going to remove him. He didn't see the blessing of generational legacy; he saw his competition. Insecure leaders are fearful leaders; they see other people as competitors not as assets.

These areas Saul dealt with were a consequence of his internal world being out of order. He was anointed and called by God, but he still lived in insecurity. He still was afraid, and it was because his soul, his internal world, was completely in disarray.

There is a Saul nature in all of us that must be crucified. Whether it's big or small, that nature is in every human being, and it must be crucified.

Saul was driven. He was highly functional and a problem solver, a type A personality, a strong leader, and highly gifted. He was called, yet he was eventually disqualified because he could never surrender to the place of real peace and rest in his internal world and just trust God.

Now, David was a man after God's heart. He was chosen and anointed. But the Bible shows us that David's internal world was also not in order. David had a major lust issue. David was a murderer; he had too much blood on his hands to build the temple, so it had to be passed down to his son, Solomon. David did not know when it was time to put the sword down and rest. David didn't know how to correct his sons when they needed correction.

This was probably due to Saul's spiritual fathering of David. He wanted to swing the pendulum so far opposite in the other direction that he saw correction as heavy. He said, "I'm not going to be like that. So, I'm just not going to correct anyone." And then he had a son who slept with his daughter, and he didn't correct it. We know that Absalom rose, and David was the cause of Absalom's issues. All these were a result of David's internal world, his soul.

When you have leaders that won't confront, or correct, that's where you give room for Jezebel or Absalom spirits. Those things start to rise because they say, "Well, if you're not going to do it, I'm going to do it." You leave room for these kinds of spirits to start operating in people.

Now let's compare Saul with John the Baptist and his well-managed inner man.

Now in the fifteenth year of the reign of Tiberius Caesar, Pontius Pilate being governor of Judea, Herod being tetrarch of Galilee, his brother Philip tetrarch of Iturea and the region of Trachonitis, and Lysanias tetrarch of Abilene, while Annas and Caiaphas were high priests, the word of God came to John the son of Zacharias in the wilderness. And he went into all the region around the Jordan, preaching a baptism of repentance for the remission of sins. Luke 3:1-3 NKJV

That's the emergence of John on the scene. Nobody knew who this man was. He was a wild and crazy preacher with camel's hair clothes. He ate locusts and wild honey. He liked the woods. I like him.

John wasn't a man who was given a job. He was a man who lost his job. John emerged on the scene and had a powerful ministry that was exploding. People everywhere knew who John the Baptist was. That's all they were talking about in Israel, this John the Baptist and his ministry. "Have you heard of John? Have you heard this man preach?" It would have been rumbling throughout the city of Jerusalem. Thousands of people were coming to hear him preach. But John saw Jesus coming and he said, "Behold, the Lamb of God who takes away the sin of the world." The heavens opened after he baptized Jesus; Jesus was anointed. And in one moment, everyone left John and started following Jesus, except for a few disciples and a few loyal people.

As a leader, you've got to ask yourself, "How do you think that would make you feel?" You're on the mountain; everybody's praising your name, you are the man, and you're seeing transformation. Then you know that this is the Messiah, and your calling is to prepare the way for Him.

I wonder if there was anything in John's heart that he had to wrestle with. You must wonder what the shift from him to Jesus would do to him.

However, John understood stewardship. Stewardship is doing a really good job at what we've been given. John understood that to steward is to properly manage something on behalf of someone. John knew that the crowd leaving him to follow Jesus was never his crowd in the first place. How different was that from the driven Saul, who assumed he owned the throne in Israel, and he could do whatever he wished?

Just think about what you're managing—students, crowds, people, companies, careers, spiritual gifts, teams, finances, campuses, locations, worship teams, etc.—are these owned or managed? Called people consider the moment, but chosen people do not.

In addition to understanding stewardship, John knew who he was. Awareness of identity is so important—you must know who you are. Those who wrestle with who they are outwardly show and display they really don't know who they are inwardly. On the journey of discovering your identity, it's important for you to recognize who you are.

For example, I know that I'm not a worship leader, and I also know that my gifting doesn't lie in a lot of other areas either. I was talking with a good friend of mine recently who is in a different lane in the body of Christ than me, and I began to share openly with him, and he said something that stood out. He said, "I can go and do all these things and exhaust myself, but I just really hit the point in my life that I know my lane. And I'm going to be so much more effective being in my lane, and it's more effective to the whole body of Christ at large when I'm in my lane."

However, sometimes as we set out to do the things we feel led to do, exhaustion can come along with fatigue and disappointment.

I've been down this road before; I started leading out of the arm of the flesh, not the spirit, and it's just not healthy. That's why it's important to know who you are and what you're called to do as well as know what you're *not* called to do.

I see this especially in worship leaders, where a worship leader has a drive to be a famous individual. The worship culture is such a blessing and a curse at the same time because of how we run in Western Christianity. On stage, the lights, the crowd, it all becomes superstar focused and hero-oriented, and it's in the worship community I see this behaviour the most.

I watch a lot of people have that ambition who want to be in that lane, and they're probably not even called to make an album. They might not be skilled enough to do that. But in their mind, there's pressure, worldly pressure. Instead of just saying, "I'm called to sing and give glory to God", they feel the need to be successful in the eyes of the world.

I'm not going to get my identity through a microphone. I can't get my identity from someone praising me or telling me how great I did today. You have to know who you are. If you don't know who you are, then those things will crush you. And you will drive, fight, and be miserable on the inside if you don't obtain those things.

John the Baptist did not care about that. Thousands of people left him, and he was okay.

Now this is the testimony of John, when the Jews sent priests and Levites from Jerusalem to ask him, "Who are you?" He confessed, and did not deny, but confessed, "I am not the Christ." And they asked him, "What then? Are you Elijah?" He said, "I am not." "Are you the Prophet?" And he answered, "No." Then they said to him, "Who are you, that we may give an answer to those who sent us? What do you say about yourself?" He said: "I am 'The voice of one crying in the wilderness: "Make straight the way of the Lord,"' as the prophet Isaiah said." John 1:19-23 NKJV

The priests in that culture were a religious system. Every religious system is always looking for the next 'one'. Who's the next worship leader, who's the next preacher? John said, "I have a voice." One of John's reasons for success in his private world was that he had parents who had an extraordinary sensitivity.

Think about this. You have a child and your history with that child is that you had a prophetic word or a dream in your heart. That's not John's parents' case. A literal angel showed up and told them they were going to have a child. They had to name him John. And his father was mute for nine months. There's a history.

They would have parented their child a little bit differently. They knew this child was called of God. They were very sensitive to who he was while he was growing. Zachariah, John's father, would have revealed that identity to him constantly. That would have helped create his soul in a healthy way; that would have helped create stability in his heart. Growing up, he would have been constantly told, "Do you know who you are? I had an angel come and tell me and I went mute for nine months! You better get it together."

There would have been that kind of declaration over him every day of his life, about who he was because of the prophetic journey that his parents had leading up to his birth. That would have helped John to know who he was.

John also possessed an unwavering sense of purpose in life. Another look at John's remarkable response to his interrogators will reveal that he understood the purpose of his activity as a forerunner to Christ. There would have been those who questioned him regarding his feelings about the growing popularity of Jesus. He likened his purpose to a bridegroom,

He who has the bride is the bridegroom; but the friend of the bridegroom, who stands and hears him, rejoices greatly because of the bridegroom's voice. Therefore this joy of mine is fulfilled. John 3:29 NKJV

John was able to experience great joy in his purpose, knowing part of his purpose was pointing people to Jesus.

Likewise, a healthy inner man should also possess an unwavering sense of purpose in life. What if, in ministry, we have this idea that it's not about how big we can get? What if we can find joy in sending out others into their purpose? John understood this concept well.

Ultimately, a healthy individual always walks in commitment to the principle of release. What we call the principle of release is one of the greatest fulfillments of a burning man or woman to pass the torch to someone else, especially the next generation.

I find it fascinating that I've heard many make comments on how they're not "being used" in church. "Use me," they say. "They don't see the talent on my life."

I've pastored long enough to see people pick up their families and leave because one family member did not feel like they were being used. Their kids are on fire for God, their spouse is on fire for God, and then one family member says, "You know what? I'm not being used the way that they should use me, and they'll approve everybody else," and run. They don't understand the principle of release. What about your kids? Ministry is more than just being used. If my kids grow up and don't love God, and don't know the things of the Spirit, I fail as a dad.

I remember the first time I watched my daughter, Micaiah, go to the altar. She was on her knees. She was weeping at the altar with her hands lifted up, and the Lord whispered to me, "Right now, you are a rich man."

Rich. I didn't have much money at the time, but I was a rich man. That's what it's about: the principle of release. It's saying, "I'm going to lay my life down for someone else. I can be a stepping stone for them to launch into what God has for them."

As believers and leaders, especially leaders, we must obtain from a place of peace and right order in our inner world. Because the private world is the interior of you as a person, your mind, will, and emotions. If my private world is in order, it will be because I've made a daily determination to see time as God's gift and worthy of careful investment.

Ask a rich man, a wealthy man, at the end of his life, "What would you want right now?" He would say, "If I can go back and do it all over again one more time, the most valuable thing is time. You can't buy it. It's the most valuable thing."

The difference between healthy and unhealthy believers is the ability to manage this internal world. I'm talking about the interior part of you, to live in peace and rest and to constantly flow from that place. To not be like a Saul who is insecure, fearful, and going to fight his way to the top, biting and working the system. Having to hang with the right people, being with the right crowd, wondering if you can get in close enough with *that* person, maybe you'll get your foot in the door...

No.

That's not the Kingdom. That's the world—that's the world type of peace. Joy in the inner world is rest. That's where Jesus lives. That's His address.

Questions for reflection:

Am I more like Saul or John? What is the state of my inner man, and what does God want me to do about it?

Lesson 10 Stop and Sit by the Well

TJ Green

Sometimes we overlook the humanness of Jesus, and we expect Him to have no issues. But He was having a human experience. It's refreshing and healing to see Jesus go through things that we go through.

And Jacob's well was there. So Jesus, tired as He was from His journey, sat down by the well. It was then about the sixth hour (noon). John 4:6 AMP

Jesus was weary from the journey, and it was only noon. It was only halfway through the day. We can expect that if Jesus got weary on the journey in ministry, we will get weary too.

The amazing thing is that while He was tired and resting at the well, an amazing opportunity presented itself. A woman arrived. Jesus was tired, maybe He didn't have a lot to pour out. He said to Photina, "If you knew who I was, you'd ask Me for a drink because I'm the well that never runs dry."

Photina went into the city and said, "I had an encounter with God." Jesus, even though He was tired and weary, was still the Prince of Peace.

Jesus ministered to Photina and it turned into extended meetings. I don't know if that's what Jesus was wanting at that moment. But the whole region went into extended meetings.

There's the notion that He was tired, yet inside Him was a well that never ran dry. We can be physically tired, we can be mentally and emotionally overwhelmed but still have the recognition that there's still a well, there's still a river of life that never runs dry, flowing out of us.

I wonder about my moments of being tired and exhausted, when they've turned into some of the best ministry moments. It wasn't my ability. It wasn't my strength. It wasn't my energy. It was me being a vessel and allowing God to move through me. There was no striving in that mode because I didn't have anything left.

So, if you get weary, stop and sit by the well, because He is the well that never runs dry.

Come to Me, all who are weary and heavily burdened [by religious rituals that provide no peace], and I will give you rest [refreshing your souls with salvation]. Matthew 11:28 AMP

My days and my weeks are ordered by my lists. My job list rarely gets done. My list grows and the next day I have a bigger list. I tend to get stressed out, especially if I'm ministering multiple times. Sometimes I even take that home with me. I'm overwhelmed. I've got the pull of people. I've got the pull of ministry, and then I come home, and I am weary. I come into my environment at home, and I bring into it that overwhelmed feeling.

It's interesting that the Hebrew culture practices Shabbat. Shabbat means cease and stop. The Hebrew greeting blessing is Shabbat Shalom, which means stop in rest.

Thus the heavens and the earth were completed in all their vast array. By the seventh day God had finished the work he had been doing; so on the seventh day he rested from all his work. Then God blessed the seventh day and made it holy, because on it he rested from all the work of creating that he had done. Genesis 2:1-3 NIV

Work was a blessing. For six days there was work; work was a blessing, but toil and striving was a curse. God accomplished the work. He finished the work and then He reveled in it. He sat and enjoyed the finished work. On the seventh day if we stop and practice Shabbat, we're mirroring God. We're stopping and enjoying the finished work.

God, He's done. He completed at the cross a finished work in us. When we stop and enjoy the finished work on the seventh day, we're mirroring God.

When we stop and rest on the seventh day, it can be a celebration of the liberation of our work. Our work is not the center of the universe. In Exodus, there were slaves of brickmaking, and the first time God gave them a commandment, there was an instruction to Shabbat.

It's interesting because 70 chapters into the Torah, God finally gave the Israelites some instruction to stop and rest. They'd been in a system of slavery, where part of their identity was to work and make bricks, and God said, "Stop."

After the law was established, the Israelites celebrated by releasing people. On the seventh year, slaves were released. They celebrated and released people in the year of Jubilee which was the seventh year of the seventh year. People's debts were forgiven. It was finished. It was erased. It was completed; they were free from it.

There were all these tensions that Jesus had with the religious leaders when he started healing on the Sabbath. That was a big contentious issue.

Chris Frost shared a story with me about the Sabbath. He was in Germany on a trip with Bethel, and he was teaching on healing. He was going to bed one night and felt like Jesus said, "You know, I often heal on the Sabbath. And when the people got angry, it was because they thought it was out of work, but I did it out of rest."

It was more like gifts of the Spirit speaking. Prophecy and preaching, and ministry of healing, come out of a place of rest. That's what God flows through.

Questions for reflection:

In what area of your life is God teaching you to rest? Is this an area you need to learn more from Jesus' example?

Lesson 11 Identity

Heather Paton

I feel in culture right now there's a crisis of identity, and whenever the Holy Spirit does something, the enemy comes in a mimicking spirit to mock it. Jesus makes this statement to His disciples several times in the New Testament: "Watch and pray."

Watch and pray, which is interesting because we always tell people to close their eyes when they pray. I think this started as children to keep us from being distracted, but watching means our eyes need to be open.

I remember when we were running a youth camp and revival had been pouring out. The kids didn't want to play sports. They didn't want to do anything. They just wanted to be in the presence of God. There was a girl who was about 13 and said she really had a heart for intercession and prayer. Most kids at 13 years old don't make statements like that unless they really mean it. Jamie pulled her up to the side of the altar and said to look, to keep her eyes open and to perceive what the Spirit was doing in the room. She started seeing things in the Spirit and eventually was on the floor weeping, creating a puddle of tears on the cement floor in front of her. She was called in intercession and until that moment, didn't fully understand it.

Paul constantly says, "Be watchful and pray." What I see in this culture right now is a massive identity crisis. We keep saying, "Lord, I want beloved identity. I know that you love me," and yet, the more we pray, the more we struggle with identity. Even seasoned leaders struggle with it. I think that's the part where I'm saying, "God, if the church doesn't get it, how are the lost ever going to get it? Because we're still struggling with position and identity."

I see a culture sitting outside of school every day. A good percentage of them are struggling with what sexuality they are, what pronoun they are, and it's creeping into the church.

I really feel like the Lord is saying, "Be watchful, and pray to know who you are in Christ."

I feel really agitated in my spirit today. My heart is broken when looking at society because they're so lost. And if we're a mess when we have a Saviour, I don't know how everyone else who doesn't is going to get it, until we really take hold of our identity.

In church, we gather, and it's fun and exciting, but we have no awareness of what's happening around us. What's happening in the school system? What's happening in workplaces? We're so consumed about what God is going to do in and through us that we forget that there's people dying all around us.

Let's stop asking, "Where's my next assignment? What am I going to do for You? Where am I going to go? Who am I going to speak to? What's my next position?"

Instead, in our prayer time, in that secret place, ask, "Lord, what are You doing on the earth today? What is it that Your Father is doing that I need to partner with to bring chaos back into order?"

I feel like the Lord is saying in this season to know our identity. Knowing that we are secure, knowing that we do have a plan, and we do have a seat at the table. But He's called us to do more than just magnify our gift or talent. He's called us to seek and to save the lost.

Christ, when He went to the garden of Gethsemane with His disciples said, "Watch and pray." I feel right now the Lord saying, "Watch and pray. What's going on around you? What's going on with your kids? What's going on in your communities? What's going on in your city beyond what God's doing in church?"

People are getting saved and set free, but as we go through the week, it's really having an ear to hear what the Spirit is saying, to watch and pray. Where is it that He needs us to serve? Where is it that we need to jump in and bring hope, life, and identity back to a culture that's in complete chaos?

People need hope, they need Jesus. There's a whole group of people outside of the walls of the church who need to hear the gospel. We need to be awakened to the signs of the times. There's an identity crisis on Earth. People need to be awakened to righteousness and who they are in Christ.

Questions for reflection:

How has the enemy attacked your identity? What areas is God leading you into to minister to people who don't know who they are?

Around the Table

Lesson 12 When You Succeed at Your Life's Call

Tracy Belford

When my daughter, Glory, and her fiancé, picked a wedding date, I was so excited. This was the best thing ever.

Then the reality hit me that my daughter was leaving home. When a kid moves out, that's one thing, but when they get married, they're never coming back. Now she is attached to someone else. She doesn't belong to me anymore in that sense.

Since then, I've been working through it with Jesus. Nobody tells you that something as wonderful as your child getting married is going to cause so much pain and so much change.

After that, I realized I have had a belief that we often share with young moms, "This is your life's call to raise your children." It's something we talked about in the church when I was raising my kids; how important parenthood is and how important it is to raise your children in the Lord. That this is your purpose, and this is your destiny.

I've really embraced all those things. It was amazing to create legacy by raising my kids. It's not that I haven't done other things, it's simply that I always perceived raising my children to be the most important thing I would ever do.

What happens when they leave? What happens when you finish raising them? When we tie our call to something like parenting, and then our kids grow up, their lives change, they move on. What happens when your call is tied to something so external like that, and then it's gone?

I've been thinking about that, not just in relation to me, but in relation to lots of other people. What does it mean for all the seniors out there who don't have kids at home or don't have a career or don't have ministry? What does it mean for people who retire? What about, for example, all the years people have been praying and talking about Roe versus Wade? This was their life's call to have it overturned. Then it got overturned. Now what?

Now what do you do when your purpose has been fulfilled? What does it mean if your call was to bring a revival to a nation and you do it? What comes after? What if your call was to lead people into freedom and worship and you succeed? What if your call was to disciple people and then they're discipled? What happens when you succeed at your life's call?

That's a very big life question.

I got married a week after my 20th birthday. And we got pregnant with my son, Jacob, three days later. I have been a mom for my entire adult life. I homeschooled my kids for 17 years. It was a call, and it was hard but worthwhile. But that season has ended.

What does our life look like now? What does the daily stuff look like; how do we cook for two of us? How does this change our free time? How does it change how we minister? How does this change who we are in this phase?

Every time I think I know who I am, the Lord shows me something new. I realized that I just don't really know anything at all. That's the beauty of beloved identity—that we keep going until we die.

We're never going to be fully in beloved identity until we're dead. And even then, I wonder maybe if He's just going to keep showing us when we're in heaven.

In this season, I reread Tony Stoltzfus' book *The Calling Journey*. It points out that most people don't arrive in fulfillment in their call until they're much older. Even 10 years ago, I thought I should have it all together. I thought I should have all the things in place to be who God made me to be.

But when you have a look at this book, you'll notice fulfillment of your call doesn't come until you've made a long journey with the Lord.

How did Joseph and Moses and all the great people of faith in the Bible walk through their callings? They went through mountains and valleys.

I don't want to be in a valley. I want to be in the high places, but with Jesus that's not how our journey works. We must go through the valleys. That's where the growth is. That's where we are established. That's where we get into what our life's call is and refine our life's message.

In our timelines, there are life transitions where leaders take on the full mantle of their calling identity, moving from doing to being where we develop a healthy detachment from our call, where it's okay if we never do what we're called to do. Yet at the same time, we're okay if God takes us there. Learn to be ok with doing it or not, so long as we are with Jesus.

The point is not to close our hearts. If it's just me and Jesus for the rest of my life, and I never accomplish anything and I never do anything, it's ok.

I talked about how my call and how my life has changed now that my external circumstances of not having children at home has changed everything. There are so many external circumstances that affect us in a myriad of ways. The success of our calling was not one that I expected to throw me off. I didn't expect success to cause me to break. But sometimes it is not our failure that breaks us, it is our success.

Now I get the joy of spending time with the Lord, establishing what He says about my call. I don't believe that I am done; I don't believe my greatest days are behind me. I believe there is so much more, and now that my attention has shifted, I have the rest of my life to figure it out with Him.

Questions for reflection:

What are some ways that your call has changed based on external circumstances? What is something that's outside of you that has changed what's inside of you? How have you handled the success of your call?

Lesson 13 Time Management

Chris Mathis

Think about all our possessions, how we live our lives chasing down happiness, retirements, and vacation time. Nothing is wrong with these things in the right context, but the older I get, the more I realize that my priorities have begun to change. The older I get; I start to realize that time is actually way more valuable.

I know I'm still fairly young, but when I turned 39, I thought I was only turning 38. I was in Winnipeg and people were asking me, "Hey, how old are you turning?" and I replied, "38." And then it hit me when I started doing the math—I realized I was turning 39! I was mad. I felt like a year had just been stolen from my life.

That's what got me thinking about this subject on time management; how I could never get that year back.

I can never get last year back or the year before then. In life, there's a lot of things we can get back that we lose. For example, if I lose a car, I can get another one.

As I'm pushing 40, time is more on the forefront of my mind because it is way more valuable to me than it used to be. When I was in my twenties, even my thirties, I was more 'go with the flow'. Now, I'm realizing that time is extremely valuable.

How many of you feel like you struggle with managing time? Do you ever feel like there's not enough time in the day to accomplish everything? You're having to balance things like leadership, family life, children, date nights, ministering to people in the church, recreation, and vacation; these are all things we need to balance.

If we don't balance our priorities and manage our time well, unmanaged time will always flow towards your weakness. Everyone's weaknesses are different. For some, it may be sitting on the couch watching TV for ten hours at a time while eating chips. For others, it may be spending money shopping. I can walk around Cabela's for hours at a time and spend a lot of money if I don't manage that part of my life.

I teach new believers that idle time is their enemy. I know when I was a new Christian, I made sure that every hour of the day was occupied. There was no idle time in my life. I was serving, I was giving, and I was always making sure I was busy doing something. Given my past, I needed to stay busy. I needed a schedule in my life. Bishop Kyle Searcy helped me do this.

Even later, as I was beginning to minister, I noticed something about Bishop Kyle. He had a little laminated calendar with the days of the week and within each day, every hour slot was filled with something. He kept it with him in his pocket: 7-9 am was prayer, 9-10 am was planning the day, 10-11 am had meetings, 11-12 pm was lunch, etc. I was so intrigued by that calendar. I started doing what he did, and it helped me learn how to manage my time.

Successful people do this. If you ever get around a successful businessperson, every hour of the day is accounted for. There's not just this free-for-all, go with the flow attitude. Successful people don't live their lives that way and if you look at any successful person, in business and/or the Kingdom, they don't live their lives that way.

That's an area of my life I want to grow in.

Laziness casts one into a deep sleep, and an idle person will suffer hunger. Proverbs 19:15 NKJV

But we command you, brethren, in the name of our Lord Jesus Christ, that you withdraw from every brother who walks disorderly and not according to the tradition which he received from us. For you yourselves know how you ought to follow us, for we were not disorderly among you; 2 Thessalonians 3:6-7 NKJV

Paul is telling believers to stay away from other believers who are idle, who are going nowhere, doing nothing with their lives, or not managing their time.

In addition, unmanaged time will come under the influence of dominant or needy people in my world.

How many of you have needy people in your world? How about dominant people? Just as God loves you and has a plan for your life, so do dominating people.

This was a lesson I had to learn as a young pastor. When we planted our first church, I was 26, which was way too young. But I didn't know that, and I gave myself to everyone, all the time. For anyone in the church, I'd run to meet their need, and all the needy people would always be right there, always with a never-ending need.

Eventually, I found myself feeling burned out. One time, Bishop Kyle had to step in because I was so burned out. He said, "Listen, you need a sabbatical. You're taking six weeks off. Go somewhere and stop. You're chasing down people that are not even going to be here in two years."

Leaders, the reality is that the majority of the neediest people who want the most of your time won't even be around in a year. That is a crazy thing! And yet, we as leaders can get caught up in a mode of trying to please them and meet their needs.

We have nothing that we can give them other than Jesus. Needy people can control your time without realizing it, and you think you're doing God a service by helping them. But it's people that are stealing your time. We must be careful and aware of that, especially if we have a need to be needed. Our unmanaged time will always flow towards people that are dominant.

Unmanaged time will surrender to the demands of all emergencies. Not everything that cries the loudest is the most urgent thing. Usually, the thing that screams the loudest is not important at all.

If you think about all the problems in the last year or two, that were screaming loud in the moment, the ones where you dropped everything and ran to, can you even remember what those problems were? Most of us can't even remember what the actual issue was today. Yet at that moment, it seemed like it was the number one priority because it was unmanaged time.

If you have unmanaged time, you will surrender that to the demands of all emergencies. For example, just recently, I had a text from someone that said, "I really need to see you today. I've got a ton of things I need to run by you. I know it's your first day back in the office. Can I come in this afternoon?" I replied, "No, it's my first day back in the office. I have a lot of stuff I need to catch up on. Why don't you shoot me an email?" They replied, "Okay, thanks." Because I have a history with that person, I know that individual will say something like that, come in and see me, and it'll be something completely unnecessary. And then they'll sit there for 30 minutes and say, "Hey, man, what did you do for the last three weeks?"

That's where you must take control of your time.

If you want to recapture your time, you must know your personal rhythms of effectiveness. Each and every one of us has a rhythm that causes us to be effective. And every person's rhythm is going to be different.

I'm effective when my house is clean. I'm effective in the morning. I'm effective when I can have devotion first thing in the morning and then plan my day after that. I am most focused then, and I can think more clearly when it's silent. That's usually the time that I give the Lord, and I know that about myself.

I must have a planned-out strategy of how to use my time. Again, this goes back to the detailed calendar. I have my calendar in my phone that plans and schedules all my meetings. I make sure that there's also time that is not for meetings. I'll put a block of 'no meetings' on certain days where they'll be dedicated to family or something similar. You may not be as detailed as Bishop Kyle, who has a very detailed calendar, but you still need to plan your time.

Jesus knew the calendar of His Father in heaven, and He didn't do anything unless He saw his Father do it first. He understood that with every person and appointment He had, it was essential He had good time management. He would leave the crowds and go to the one. This was time management. Jesus would often draw away and pray. That's also good time management. Jesus wasn't moved by the ministry demands. That's good time management.

Ultimately, you need to budget time and command it. Take command of your time in advance. Don't wait until the last moment. You are the one who decides what to do with your time, so command it instead of letting it run you.

Questions for reflection:

How does unmanaged time flow towards your weakness? Are there any needy or dominant people in your life that you need to be a better time steward with? And what does that look like? When and how are you most effective?

Lesson 14 I Wanna Be Me, Not You

Paulina Guinez

This past year the Lord has been teaching me to walk out authenticity. I've been finding out who I am, what my voice sounds like, what my walk looks like, and how He has made me. It has been terrifying and uncalculated, but the most freeing experience.

According to the dictionary, authenticity is genuine, of undisputed origin, pure, real, true, dependable, reliable, and faithful. The opposite of authenticity is fake, corrupt, unreliable, and doubtful.

In the world, authenticity has turned into filtered moments, and reality shows that are scripted and dishonest. We live in a culture where people look to worldly gods to tell them who they are, what they should look like, and how they should sound and express themselves.

In this broken world, many people are suffering from mental health issues, believing they need to hide their true selves. People are learning how to numb themselves, dissociate, and create aliases and characters to cope and survive day to day. Many have never met their true selves. In contrast, the Lord, the very maker of our DNA, has been singing who we are over us for generations.

"Your lives light up the world. For how can you hide a city that stands on a hilltop? And who would light a lamp and then hide it in an obscure place? Instead, it's placed where

everyone in the house can benefit from its light. So don't hide your light! Let it shine brightly before others, so that your commendable works will shine as light upon them, and then they will give their praise to your Father in heaven." Matthew 5:14-16 TPT

In the Bible notes, it explains that the Aramaic word for light is often used as a metaphor for teachings that bring enlightenment and revelation into the hearts of men.

Light also represents the presence of God, and Jesus is the light of God within us. The Lord was showing me that the more we know Him and spend time with Him, the deeper the revelation we receive of Him. The deeper revelation we receive of Him, the deeper the revelation we will receive of ourselves. By knowing Him we ultimately learn who we are, how we are supposed to sound, and how to act. We gain confidence in the truth, and as revelation moves into our hearts and deep within us, we begin to function in our real identity and true authenticity.

"So don't hide your light, let it shine brightly before others so that the commendable things you do will shine as light upon them, and then they will give praise to your Father in heaven." Matthew 5:16 TPT

We weren't made to hide in corners. If you put a light in the corner, it'll only reflect within that corner. But if you put it in the center, it radiates more light into the room.

Imagine if every Christian functioned authentically, there would be no room for darkness to dwell. When we function in the understanding of who we are in Him, we shine brighter, and as the Scripture says, people will praise the Lord for the light that we bring. We are doing a disservice to the body when we are not functioning as our authentic selves, hiding in the corner of rooms.

Authenticity does not look like perfection. It looks like failing, getting back up, boundaries, discovering, learning, maturing, apologizing and adjusting, having pure motives on the road of discovery and being okay with not fitting what's trending or being within a set timeline. We are designed to outlast the world and whatever is trending within it. The world needs to see something different, something unheard of, unique, and that is us being fully authentic, honest, and real. It's attractive—like light in a dark room, you can't help but go to it.

I find as you know who you are in Christ, it becomes easier to love and celebrate others, and I believe this is because you learn to love and celebrate yourself. Allowing those around you to shine their lights becomes easier and provides more light in the environment to see clearly. I truly desire to see more young people like me, and people in every generation, experience the freedom of living a lifestyle of authenticity.

Questions for reflection:

How do we encourage and celebrate authenticity and identity in our current culture? To ourselves? To those we minister to and those around us.

Around the Table

Lesson 15 Empowerment & Development

Des Belford

Within Summit, we are asking the question, "How do we go about the process of developing leaders?"

I've been really wrestling with that. The two words that I have been dwelling on are *empowerment* and *development*.

How do we empower new leaders? How do we develop leaders? The words *empowerment* and *development* are synonymous, and they work in congruence with each other. They flow together, and they're a key part in the discipleship process.

How do we see this in the Bible? How did Jesus empower and develop His disciples?

One day as Jesus was walking along the shore of the Sea of Galilee, he saw two brothers—Simon, also called Peter, and Andrew—throwing a net into the water, for they fished for a living. Jesus called out to them, "Come, follow me, and I will show you how to fish for people!" And they left their nets at once and followed him. Matthew 4:18-20 NLT

Jesus called Peter into empowerment. Jesus said, "I will make you fishers of men." He called Peter into discipleship first. But then immediately Jesus said, "I will make you fishers of men for God." That's the beginning of the empowerment phase. "Here you go. This is your calling. This is what you're going to do." But Jesus didn't release him into being a fisher of men, because it required a development process first.

Think about learning to drive. A teen can watch YouTube and think they can drive a car. But just watching YouTube is not the same as actually driving a car. Instead, we can take the teen to the parking lot and let the teen try to back up the car. We start the process of empowerment by saying, "Let's go practice in the parking lot."

After the teen can successfully back the car up, we then say, "Here's the keys. You can back the car up anytime you want." That empowers the teen to back up, and now he knows he can do something, but still needs to learn more.

In needing to learn more, he enters the process of development, which in this case is learning to signal and turn a corner.

In the Kingdom, empowerment is attached to authority. The process of development is the start of learning and growing. Empowerment and development are essential for church culture and community building, as we transform incomplete people into developed people.

Incomplete people are those who are looking for a place to serve but are not yet ready. Or, maybe they're brand new, overlooked, or have been empowered through other programs. These are people who have never actually been developed into a culture of sustainability and usability.

There is a process involved when taking leaders who are empowered but not fully developed. We can take them and see where they need to be developed, so they can learn and grow and be able to minister in a way that brings life.

Development requires both success and failure. Peter is one of the best examples of the development process. He had lots of awesome adventures where he said, "Hey, let me build you a house on this mountain." But it wasn't the time. "I'm going to cut your ear off, how dare you touch the Lord!" Again, it was not the time for Peter.

Then Peter called to him, "Lord, if it's really you, tell me to come to you, walking on the water." "Yes, come," Jesus said. So Peter went over the side of the boat and walked on the water toward Jesus. But when he saw the strong wind and the waves, he was terrified and began to sink. "Save me, Lord!" he shouted. Matthew 14:28-30 NLT

In the story of the storm, the disciples were rolling out onto the lake and Jesus appeared to them walking on water! They freaked out. They thought Jesus was a ghost. Peter said, "If it's really you, call me out. I'll come." Peter stepped out on the water. He had a moment of success. Then he looked down and had a moment of failure because he became afraid and started to sink. The development and empowerment process requires success and failure.

The development and empowerment process requires leaders to be invested in those that they are empowering and developing. When Peter starts to sink, we see Jesus reach out his hand and pull Peter up.

Empowerment is attached to authority, whereas development is attached to ability.

Again, empowerment is like giving my son the car keys and telling him, "You can back the car up in the driveway anytime that you want." But it takes the process of being developed through several driving lessons to be able to handle driving on the road. The empowerment comes from my authority. The development comes from my son's ability to handle a car on the road.

The process of empowerment and development requires restoration and correction. Healthy empowerment and development make room for life to happen in imperfect situations.

After breakfast Jesus asked Simon Peter, "Simon son of John, do you love me more than these?" "Yes, Lord," Peter replied, "you know I love you." "Then feed my lambs," Jesus told him. Jesus repeated the question: "Simon son of John, do you love me?" "Yes, Lord," Peter said, "you know I love you." "Then take care of my sheep," Jesus said. A third time he asked him, "Simon son of John, do you love me?" Peter was hurt that Jesus asked the question a third time. He said, "Lord, you know everything. You know that I love you." Jesus said, "Then feed my sheep. "I tell you the truth, when you were young, you were able to do as you liked; you dressed yourself and went wherever you wanted to go. But when you are old, you will stretch out your hands, and others will dress you and take you where you don't want to go." Jesus said this to let him know by what kind of death he would glorify God. Then Jesus told him, "Follow me." John 21:15-19 NLT

After Jesus had risen, there was a process of restoration for Peter, but there was also correction in the affirming. Peter was restored, but he was also corrected, and he was moving forward in that development.

Empowerment and development are intertwined in that you can't have one without the other. If you have people who are empowered doing empowered things, but they're not developed in the culture of the house and the culture of the time, they can be loose cannons. They can hurt people and cause damage. Empowerment needs to be in tandem with development, so damage doesn't happen.

In Luke 24 when Jesus was about to leave, He commissioned the disciples, blessed them, and then He left. He told them that He'd send the Holy Spirit to be with them to continue their development.

As a parent of adult children, I'm just a sounding board now. I have empowered and developed them to live adult lives. I'm no longer holding their hand saying, "Don't touch the stove. That's hot." I'm saying, "I'm going to guide you now, and you're going to be able to live your own life."

A byproduct of empowerment and development with healthy leadership is you see the expectation of return.

Around the Table

As a result of the apostles' work, sick people were brought out into the streets on beds and mats so that Peter's shadow might fall across some of them as he went by. Crowds came from the villages around Jerusalem, bringing their sick and those possessed by evil spirits, and they were all healed. Acts 5:15-16 NLT

Peter had been empowered and developed, so he was able to be successful, and to go on and do what Jesus did.

Questions for reflection:

What are your go-to empowerment and development strategies for leaders or for people you are leading? What have been some of your most impactful moments in life of being empowered and developed?

Lesson 16 The Business of Revival

TJ Green

The Hebrew definition of Adam's name is 'a bloody dirt clod' or 'rendered dirt'. I think that keeps us humble, but it also is amazing because the DNA of God is on the inside of us. It's like a perfect composition of the dust and the divine, and when we yield to the dust, we fall. When we yield to our earthly nature, we enter into sin because we forget who we are. When we walk in who we were created to be, we are not walking in sin. We're walking in our divine nature.

When Adam bowed down to things he was supposed to have dominion and authority over, he fell. We always fall when we bow down to something we're supposed to have dominion over. We shouldn't because we were created in the image and likeness of God.

Sometimes, we have to get a job done, and it can become policy over people very quickly. We may forget our whole purpose is to create a place to facilitate personal encounters. This is us being the family of God.

We're facilitating, administrating, and working so people can have a personal face to face encounter with God. We need to be as kind as Yahweh, and when we're not, it is probably an indication that we don't see ourselves in the image and likeness of God. If we cannot see other people or treat other people in the image and likeness of God, we aren't acting like Him. Sin happens whenever love gets violated. When we treat anybody less than the image and likeness of God, we're forgetting who we are, and what God put in us. It really bothers me when I see people being treated poorly.

I want to make this personal, as our family went through so much abuse in Jamaica, because it was always policy over people. They didn't care about our son, Dax, who we were trying to adopt. They said, "This is our policy, which was set in place to protect people from child trafficking." It was for good reason that all these safeguards were set in place. But when the safeguards end up abusing or hurting the people, it's a problem. It's got to be people over policy, every single time.

The business of church, the business of revival is not as important as the people. God cares more about the people. Jesus says to love others as we love ourselves. I think honour flows both ways, up and down. If we're honouring people who can advance us, who can promote us, who can do something for us, is that honour really pure? Are we honouring people who are always serving? Are we honouring those in positions below us?

I think we need to understand the Kingdom of heaven. Honour always is flowing in every direction, because every one of us was created in the image and likeness of God.

We have people who are 'grace growers', those people who require a lot of grace. But the amazing thing about grace is there's always more grace. We never have enough grace.

One of the questions I ask myself is, "Is it possible to burn out if you're abiding, if you've trimmed off the stuff that God never asked you to do?"

When I was a younger pastor, pastoring was all about putting out the fires, handling all the crises. Pastor Peter Nash told me to let the fires burn. I was like, "Wait, isn't it 99% of my job to put the fires out? And then be in the presence of God the other one percent?" I would get filled up enough in the presence of God so that I could have enough energy to run around and deal with all the drama. Pastor Peter said, "I find if I just let them burn long enough, they usually die out along the way. We are not the Holy Spirit. We don't have to run around and put out everything." What a lesson for me. It was a whole new way of pastoring for me.

We need to teach people to put out their own fires. We don't have to be the fire department. Pastor Peter said, "I find if I just let things happen, if I'm not too hands on, Holy Spirit has more of a chance to move in people's lives instead of me trying to always be training them. Let it burn for a bit."

What good news, not rushing to everyone's crisis. We love people enough to let them figure it out and grow into maturity. With my son, I'm letting him figure things out on his own more instead of me doing it for him. Why? Because I want him to know how to do it if I'm not there.

Adam and Eve weren't walking around the garden with a water gun trying to water all the plants. They had a job to do, they had authority and dominion. Their primary function was to walk with God in the cool of the day. The garden took care of itself. They didn't have to water plants. The mist came up from the ground and watered the fruit of their garden. They had a function. But when they kept the primary thing in their life primary, the function almost took care of itself.

I like meditating on that because they did have a job to do. God gave them authority and dominion, but God created them and planted them in a place for their success. He put them in a perfect environment to succeed in every area of their lives. He put them in a garden where there would be a lot of fruit.

God has planted us in a garden. Our environment is set up for our success when we're in intimacy with God. When we're walking with Him in the course of the day, when we're doing the primary job, the rest will administer itself to some degree. Things will start to take care of themselves when we remember the primary goal.

My first experience with revival was one that I didn't understand. It was 30 days. We had a mist in the sanctuary. There was an actual *kabod*, a Shekinah glory, the presence of God. We could see His manifest presence, and people were getting saved every day without evangelism.

As we were hosting the presence of God, I wanted to shut it down because there was part of me that wanted control. There was part of me that wanted to administer, and there was part of me that didn't understand all of this. Was I really going to accept what I didn't understand? I had enough fear of God not to quench the Holy Spirit. That was one of the lessons.

I was the only person on staff, when after 30 days, the board said, "We need to put more safeguards in place. The kids don't have experience being the ministry team. There's bad stuff that could happen. We need to protect this thing." They wanted to micromanage it, and revival was shut down. The presence lifted; it was gone. I remember grieving, because we tried to box it, and we tried to give it a name. We tried to put badges on people who were allowed to minister. I understood that some safeguards were needed. Our reaction was a fear reaction of trying to control the situation.

Do we want a God who we can move around, or do we want a God who is fearful, awesome, amazing, and Who takes us somewhere?

Moses and all of Israel were invited up the mountain. Moses was the only one who went up the mountain. He is the archetype of success in the Old Testament. Forty days he stayed in the face of God. The people asked for a calf, which was a god that didn't move. It was stationary. It was a god that they could control. When they asked Aaron for a god to lead them, they were asking for a god that they could lead and control. Yet originally it was arranged for all of Israel to go up the mountain, to go up the summit with Moses.

Enoch lived 365 years, walking in close fellowship with God. Then one day he disappeared, because God took him. Genesis 5:23-24 NLT

This is fascinating to me because the Bible never says Enoch did anything. What did he do? Did he do anything except what Adam and Eve did in the very beginning, which was walk and talk with God?

Enoch was not the first person to walk and talk with God. Adam and Eve were. God loved it so much, someone who captured that garden experience of walking with Him in the cool of the day. Scripture also says Enoch walked and talked with God and then was no more. God took him away. That word in Hebrew is *Lakesh*. *Lakesh* is a word that is used the majority of the time for marriage. I like to say Enoch married up; he got caught up in the love of God. God loved this relationship so much that He took him right into eternity.

What did Enoch do? What legacy did he leave? What church did he build? How many people did he save? How did he grow the Kingdom of God? I don't know. But he is in Scripture forever as an example of one who walked with God.

We can never neglect the primary business of revival for anything else. We can never neglect walking and talking with God. I want to grow in desire for Jesus. I want to desire Him more than everything else. I just want Jesus; He is the one Who is revival.

Questions for reflection:

Where is God teaching you to see people in the image and likeness of God? And how are you getting caught up in the love of God lately? Are you enjoying God to the fullest?

Lesson 17 Going Through the Fire with Jesus

Tracy Belford

I've been reading a Christian psychology book called *Inside Out* by Dr Larry Crabb. In the introduction, it talks about how we as Christians tend to want to make everything look perfect. We're good, or we're fine. We don't need any help, especially in church leadership. We want everyone to think we've got it all together. And the truth is, we don't. We're just people like everybody else.

We have this great need to make it look like we've got it together because somehow that makes us more competent leaders. As I was reading this, I knew this was absolutely something that we all do. It was talking about the average Christian, even their desire to come to church and look perfect, because God forbid, they should have something broken.

It got me thinking about how often we come to church, and we pretend, or how often we come and we're not authentic.

I was thinking about when I was nineteen and in Bible college. I was on my way to pick up Des to help him move, and I had a car accident. I was driving and a car T-boned me and I spun 270 degrees. It was really traumatic. I wasn't injured super badly. I only had soft tissue damage.

But after that accident, I struggled. I grew up in church, I knew all the right things. I started asking, "God, if You love me, why did this bad thing happen?" During this first crisis of my faith, I was in Bible college. I felt I should not be having this crisis but instead, I should have it together. I was asking, "Where were You God? I thought You loved me. I thought I was Your daughter. How dare You let this happen to Your daughter." I was really mad at Him. And I struggled for months. Much of my Bible college existence was struggling with God.

"Why did this happen; I thought You loved me?" was my question until one day I read a scripture in Acts 17, which was totally unrelated. Somehow, this Scripture seriously touched my heart, and I was able to release the question and let it go. I realized I was going to face trials.

Pastor Chris Mathis has often said, "If you don't have trials, then are you really serving Jesus?" I thought to myself, "I'm not in any trials right now." I was in a good season. However, if I'm not facing trials, what am I even learning right now?

In my worst trial, when my daughter died, the Scripture that touched me most was this:

Yet what we suffer now is nothing compared to the glory he will reveal to us later. Romans 8:18 NLT

In that time, it was only helpful because I could see that there was a purpose. The fact there was suffering meant that later on something good was going to come. I couldn't see the good, and I couldn't see daylight, but I knew that He was going to do something good later.

We can rejoice, too, when we run into problems and trials, for we know that they help us develop endurance. And endurance develops strength of character, and character strengthens our confident hope of salvation. And this hope will not lead to disappointment. For we know how dearly God loves us, because he has given us the Holy Spirit to fill our hearts with his love. Romans 5:3-5 NLT

Again, it shows there's a purpose to the trial, that we develop endurance and character. I thought, "That is not enough, Jesus. I don't just want good character. There must be a better reason for this."

I was only seeing my problems in the moment. I was not seeing it long term, Kingdom eternal. The whole point of this life is eternal. And what I saw right then were just my problems.

Dear brothers and sisters, when troubles of any kind come your way, consider it an opportunity for great joy. For you know that when your faith is tested, your endurance has a chance to grow. So let it grow, for when your endurance is fully developed, you will be perfect and complete, needing nothing. James 1:2-4 NLT

I want to be perfect and complete right now. I do not want to rejoice in troubles, but trouble produces gratitude in us, and whenever we're walking around full of gratitude, people gravitate towards that. When we let the trials become our joy, it changes how people relate to us. When we are like Eeyore from *Winnie the Pooh*, no one wants to spend time with us. Growing and allowing the trouble to become joy is a hard thing.

My heart is filled with bitter sorrow and unending grief for my people, my Jewish brothers and sisters. I would be willing to be forever cursed—cut off from Christ! —if that would save them. Romans 9:2-3 NLT

Paul's heart was filled with sorrow and unending grief. If the fathers of the faith walked around with sorrow and unending grief, why do we think we have to be perfect? If he could share with all of humanity that he was filled with sorrow and grief, why are we hiding it? Why are we not being real and authentic about it?

Jesus said, "I have told you all this so that you may have peace in me. Here on earth, you will have many trials and sorrows. But take heart, because I have overcome the world." John 16:33 NLT

I always look at that Scripture and think about peace, but what about the sorrow? If we are not having trials and sorrows, why would He fill us with peace? What would be the point of the peace if we didn't need it?

Even when I walk through the darkest valley, I will not be afraid, for you are close beside me. Your rod and your staff protect and comfort me. Psalm 23:4 NLT

We need God to be near us, but we don't need Him if we're not having any trouble. If everything's great, then why do we even need God? What is the point of our salvation if we don't even need Him? We would not need the salvation. If we're self-sufficient enough to do this with our own strength, what's the point of it all? Everything we do revolves around the fact that our hearts were broken and separated from God. Our entire life, our careers here at the church, revolve around our brokenness and Him fixing our brokenness, healing it, and turning it into something beautiful.

Reading all those things makes me want to be more okay with the brokenness in me. My automatic go-to when I am suffering is to isolate. I don't want to share with anyone. I don't want anyone to know that I'm struggling. But all these Scriptures show me that brokenness is valuable and worth sharing.

The other side of the coin is that sometimes people want others to fix them instead of going to God, and that is not what I am advocating. We must go to God first. He is the only One who can fix us. But the idea that we cannot share our brokenness with others is a lie.

Questions for reflection:

What is the healthiest way you can possibly deal with trials? As a leader, do you let anyone in when you are struggling?

Around the Table

Lesson 18 Hard Truths

Jamie Paton

There are seven hard truths—which are harder truths if you are a leader. When you're somebody who doesn't have a position of influence, these truths are easier, but when you're a leader, they become a lot harder because of the responsibility that comes with them and the pressure you put on yourself.

1. First and foremost, you are not your past. You learn from your past to build a better future. Jay Haizlip says, "You're either a prisoner of your past or a pioneer of your future."

You learn one of two ways. You learn by mentor, or you learn by your mistakes. I prefer to learn by a mentor than by mistake because it's easier to listen to the advice of a mentor than it is to climb out of the hole of mistake.

Whether it's the shame that you put on yourself, the guilt, or the consequences of your mistakes, they teach you where your flaws are. They inspire success, even though you messed up or broke down. They help you in the future to bring forth success out of those same situations. Your past will shape your future. That's why it's important for you to mature. As you mature, you realize that you can think about your decisions and about the impact they are going to have on you tomorrow.

Your past also makes you stronger. Have you been made stronger by what you've walked through in your life? You might not understand what or why you've gone through it. It could be something that happened in the church, your family or friend group, or in your career. It doesn't matter; it makes you stronger. You can either let it destroy you or build you.

Your future needs you, your past doesn't. It sounds very heartless when I say it this way, but I don't have a lot of time for people who just want to live in their past. I understand that you have trauma and there's things that you walk through. I also understand that there is impact from that trauma in your lives, but people who desire to live in the trauma, who will not make the move to get out or move forward, frustrate me.

Now if somebody is struggling with something they are walking through, I absolutely help them. But I don't have time for somebody who doesn't want to help themselves.

Ultimately, you are not your past.

2. Time is precious, yet uncontrollable. Nobody has enough strength in them to hold up time or to slow it down. There will always be 24 hours in a day.

To optimize your time, you should prioritize your activities and plan your day in advance.

I've had to learn over the years to plan my day. Usually, I plan those days either in advance, or first thing in the morning. One of the greatest things I've ever heard from a mentor was: You can control your morning, but you can never control your evening. He encouraged all the leaders who sat under him to get up early to learn what it was to sacrifice a little bit of sleep. When nobody else is up—nobody is buzzing your phone or looking for you because they are asleep—you can plan for the day.

Today is the day to change your life. Mike Murdock said, "Time is the only currency in heaven that will allow you to buy other gifts." When you think of it, time is the ultimate currency.

God puts such a value on your time here. He's given you your lives. He's offered this to you. He made the sacrifice and offered Himself to you, but it's your decision how to use that time. It's your choice. It's your decision to go to Him and spend time. I realize how much value God puts on your time here on earth.

I believe that in the times you spend with God, your gifts can be honed. In those times, there's doors that open and opportunities that God gives. You don't spend time with Him so you can get from Him, yet He pours out the very opportunities you need.

3. Comparison is the thief of joy. When you sit around and compare yourselves to others, that's not fun at all.

If I begin to think I can't teach like Chris, then suddenly, I think, "Well, am I good enough then? What do I have to offer my team? I can't giggle the way that TJ does. My voice isn't as deep as Chris'." Comparison steals my joy and sense of belonging.

When will you realize that you don't own what's been given to you? You've all been given an opportunity to represent yourselves the way that God created you in the world and to use your gifts and talents to promote the Kingdom of God.

However it looks, I've got to own what's true for me and focus on my purpose. When I focus on my experiences, the things that I want to experience and the things that I have experienced, I have to own my own feelings. I must bring them in check and say, "Listen, I'm not going to do this. I'm not going to compare myself to somebody else."

If I try to do things the way Chris does, I'm going to mess it up and I will hate it. If I do things the way that I want to, then I'm good at doing them. I find more joy in that. There's peace that accompanies being able to own who I am.

Some days I want to compare myself to whoever, but the only competition that I have is staring back at me in the mirror. Day by day, I want to become a better person. Day by day, I want to become a deeper person. Day by day, I want to become a better friend. Day by day, I'm trying to compete with myself to be better than the day before.

4. This point will be a tough one for many to grab hold of, but you need to embrace judgment. No matter your outcome, you'll always be judged by somebody somewhere. How do I embrace judgment? First and foremost, let it go. Second, find your people, your tribe or those that you gel with, because there's no judgment in their hearts against you.

You need to learn from some criticism. There have been many times in my life where I've been judged, and I just want to turn it off and turn away from it. But a lot of those judgments were valid. The way people approached it was not, but the things that they pointed out were valuable.

Judgment and gossip occur when you sit around talking about somebody that you have no control over and no control on the outcome of their lives. If you're not willing to take it to the person, you're walking a fine line between judgment and gossip. But if you're willing to sit down and it becomes constructive criticism, spoken in a helpful way, then the person can grow from it.

Sometimes you need to take negative people out of your lives. How many people do you have in your lives that just bring you down? You need to tighten your circles and cut out negative people. You also need to focus on your long-term goals. If you focus on your goals, the opinions of man will never matter. If you stay true to yourself, and to God, the opinions of everybody else won't matter.

5. Failure is opportunity. Without failure, there cannot be success. Failure will bring you the ability to build resilience. It provides answers.

In the movie, *National Treasure*, Nicholas Cage quotes Thomas Edison, saying, "Thomas Edison said, "I didn't fail, I just found out 2000 ways not to build a light bulb.""

Failure gives you answers that you didn't know you needed, and it also accelerates growth. You think failure holds you back, but failure will show you the way. You can either spend a year trying to do something that's not working, or you can fail right away and move on.

Failure accelerates; it sparks opportunity and new ways of doing things. It makes you stronger and helps you to redirect your goals. Believe fully that failure is a stepping stone towards success.

6. Change is inevitable. The only certainty in life is change. It's important to keep up with change and stay active. Don't sit back. Don't say, "I know that it's going to change down the road. I'm going to stay here and wait until it changes again."

You need to stay active. You need to stay involved. Stay informed on what's going on. This is where I believe Moses failed by not listening to God when He asked him to speak to the rock instead of striking it. Moses was so involved with what was going on with his people that he took his focus off what God was doing. I believe God was showing him, trying to train him through a weak point in his life. Getting too involved and overwhelmed became a problem.

You need to stay informed on what's going on. You need to stay educated and connected to the Source, and ultimately, you need to stay open minded. That's how you can walk through change with a smile on your faces. If it doesn't challenge you, you will never change.

7. One of the hardest things is to aim for excellence, not perfection. Perfection is the killer of dreams. Perfection can cost you time. Perfection can increase anxiety. Perfection can starve your creativity. Perfection can prevent you from taking risks.

If you seek perfection, you'll never reach it. Practice makes you better, but it'll never make you perfect.

In the past, we built a beautiful house. I would go through the house and see little imperfections everywhere. But I realized this house was built by the hands of a man, who is strongly imperfect. The builder was a friend of mine, and he once said, "I have people who complain because they've got these little imperfections. The imperfections are nothing major—there's no walls out of line or anything like that—but rather little nicks on a wall somewhere, or something that wasn't painted correctly, or a little spot that was missing. People expect me to build a perfect house, but we're not building a piano, we're building your home." This conversation made me realize you can't have a perfectly built home. There's always going to be some flaw somewhere.

Later, we were living in a house that we were renovating. On the main floor, I had one of my guys working. It was supposed to be a six-week process on the house. This guy took three months. I asked, "What's going on?" He said, "Well, I'm trying to get this perfect." I said, "Dude, you're not going to get it perfect. Just do a good job. Do the best that you can." But he couldn't get over it. He kept us out of our home for another two months, and then he wanted to come back and bill us for all of his time. I said, "I'm not paying you for what you thought wasn't perfect because I told you this is the way that I want it, and to just fix it. Do as good of a job as you can and walk away because it's never going to be perfect, especially in a renovation when you're dealing with existing materials.

You're not going to be able to do what you want to do." But he just kept doing it over and over and over, buying more material, buying more paint, and buying things. But he realized he couldn't get past the place where he was. He was a perfectionist, but he could never come to that place of perfection.

I know that perfection is a struggle for many because you are presenting yourselves to the people you serve every single day and you're trying to make sure that everything is perfect. You all have your areas and you all want them to be perfect, but it will never be perfect. There's an element in there called humanity, and because you're not perfect, it will never be perfect.

I encourage you to not look for perfection but instead look to do your most excellent work.

Questions for reflection:

Which of these seven things is the hardest for you? How can you grow in that area?

Lesson 19 Living with the Robe of the Lastborn

Nikki Mathis

I was at Damon Thompson's church, and we were continuing to dive deeper into what beloved identity is and how we can operate from a seated place of authority. I heard the Lord speak to me about the role of the lastborn.

The Lord spoke to me about leading from the internal seat of confidence and knowing who you are on a level where hindrances that are subconscious are eradicated from the inside out. When it's not something you have to think about anymore, the change naturally happens. You don't have to try.

When I was working at a drug and alcohol rehab centre, I was talking to addicts that were trying to get free and I read them this book, *Celebration of Discipline: The Path to Spiritual Growth,* by Richard J. Foster. It talked about how the waves crash on the shore and naturally bring up the mire and the clay of the world and the mire and clay of our Adamic nature, of who we are in our sin.

For example, if you have a cussing problem and you are swearing all the time, you can willpower yourself to change, but you can only willpower yourself for so long. In unguarded moments when you're mad, or when your flesh takes over, the cussing in you will still come out.

Another example happens when loving difficult people. It's easy to love easy people. It's hard to love difficult people. Our Adamic nature comes out in the unguarded moments, in the parts where we don't have the patience. We might do well for six months, but what's still inside us will come out eventually because it's not really gone.

The change must happen from the inside out. Knowing who you are in Christ and allowing who you are to change your response to life and change your response to loving people is the only way. Then it becomes effortless; you're not changing or willing yourself to be good. You're just naturally good because of the seat that you're sitting in. As leaders, we continue to walk forward going deeper in beloved identity.

Have you ever been in somebody's house, and they offer you something and you say, "No, thank you" but you actually want it? You're thirsty, but you don't want to be a hassle. So, you say you're fine. You feel you're an inconvenience or not worthy of their effort.

I noticed that even in my own walk with God. It's easy to do that in the Lord's house, to act like we don't have the seat to ask for more, or we think we're too much of an inconvenience for Him. We have an innate unworthiness. It comes out of personality traits and things that we grew up believing about ourselves. This is what Jesus wants to flip.

I'm going to share some birth order personality traits. I know you may have heard these before, but I am giving context for what I'm talking about.

The firstborn personality traits: the oldest sibling will naturally be raised with a mixture of instinct and trial and error. This often causes parents to become by-the-book caregivers who are extremely attentive, stringent with rules and overly neurotic about the little things. This parenting style in turn may cause the child to become a perfectionist, always striving to please their parents.

Firstborns tend to bask in their parents' presence, which may explain why they sometimes act like mini adults. They're also prone to be diligent in wanting to excel at everything. They are used to being the leader of the pack. Firstborns often tend to be reliable, conscientious, structured, cautious, controlling, and achievers. They often have an intense fear of failure. Nothing they accomplish feels good enough and because they dread making a misstep, these kids tend to stick to the straight and narrow. They're typically inflexible, they don't like change and are hesitant to step out of their comfort zone.

Because parents give firstborns a lot of responsibility at home, whether it's helping with chores or watching over younger siblings, they can be quick to take charge and be bossy. That burden can lead to the excess stress for a child who already feels pressure to be perfect.

Middle child personality traits: when a second child comes along, parents might raise them with less of an iron fist due to their previous experience. They might also be less attentive since there are other children in their lives. Therefore, the middle child is often a people pleaser due to the lack of attention that they get compared to older siblings and younger siblings. The middle child often feels left out and a sense of, "Well, I'm not the oldest and not the youngest, so who am I?" This sort of hierarchy of floundering leads middle children to make their mark among their peers since parental attention is usually devoted to the beloved firstborn, or baby of the family. What's more, middle children are the toughest to pin down because they play off their older siblings. In general, middle children tend to possess the following birth order personality traits—they're people pleasers, somewhat rebellious, thrive on friendships, have a large social circle, and are peacemakers. Middle kids once lived as the baby of the family until a new sibling dethroned them. Unfortunately, they're often acutely aware that they don't get as much parental attention as their trailblazing, older sibling, or the beloved youngest.

That realisation can make them feel like their needs and wants are ignored. Middle kids are in a difficult position in a family because they think they're not valued. It's easy for them to be left out and get lost in the shuffle. And there is some validity to the complaint.

The youngest child's personality traits: the youngest child tends to be the most free-spirited due to their parents' increasingly laissez-faire attitudes in their third, fourth, or fifth time around. As a result, they're fun loving, uncomplicated, manipulative, outgoing, attention seeking and self-centered. Lastborns take risks. They're more likely to move out of the house the earliest. They have a lens that they are loved, accepted, and can do anything.

What is the main cause in all these mindsets? We are all parented by human beings. And, as a parent, even though I was aware of the birth order traits, it's something I couldn't avoid because of how I was growing as a parent. And as human parents, we obviously have failures. We obviously have fears. We obviously are stumbling through this.

When I look at why the lastborn feels so loved, it is because as parents, we're more relaxed and we're more confident. We aren't parenting out of fear anymore. The last born feels like they're loved. They feel like everybody loves them.

The cool thing about God is that He is the ultimate Father. He doesn't parent out of fear. He knows exactly how to parent with confidence. He wants every one of His kids to have the mentality of the lastborn identity. He wants all of them to feel like they can do anything. They can be risk-takers and there's nothing that can stop them because they're loved, and God, their Father, is going to back them up.

We have a perfect Father who parents from confidence, not fear. Our Father overrides our human parenting. He overrides the lack that my parents gave me. He fills in the gaps. He comes in, and He fixes the things that they messed up. The Father wants us to walk in that lastborn confidence with no insecurity.

If you think about sitting at a table and being afraid to eat all the things, you might think, "I'll just take the small portion that's given to me, and I'll drink my water because it's what's given to me. I don't want to seem greedy; I don't want to look a certain way. So, I'm going to take this small portion."

My lastborn will eat everybody's food. She'll go to somebody's house and ask for food. She's not ever going to wait for them to offer, she's just going to boldly ask for it.

"So the young son set off for home. From a long distance away, his father saw him coming, dressed as a beggar, and great compassion swelled up in his heart for his son who was returning home. The father raced out to meet him, swept him up in his arms, hugged him dearly, and kissed him over and over with tender love. "Then the son said, 'Father, I was wrong. I have sinned against you. I could never deserve to be called your son. Just let me be—' "The father interrupted and said, 'Son, you're home now!'

"Turning to his servants, the father said, 'Quick, bring me the best robe, my very own robe, and I will place it on his shoulders. Bring the ring, the seal of sonship, and I will put it on his finger. And bring out the best shoes you can find for my son. Let's prepare a great feast and celebrate. For my beloved son was once dead, but now he's alive! Once he was lost, but now he is found!' And everyone celebrated with overflowing joy. Luke 15:20-24 TPT

As sons, we can come with the mentality, "I don't deserve to be more than just a slave in your house. I've sinned, I'm a human being and I've made mistakes. I don't do all the things I'm supposed to do." We disqualify ourselves because we think the Father is looking at us with disapproval.

This can affect us as leaders because we become controlling and insecure as leaders. We can pull people to ourselves for fulfillment instead of pulling them into the Lord.

We are trying to raise up believers who want to press into the Lord, for His voice and His direction over their lives— for confidence and for security. I don't want to be everybody's super spiritual mom so that I have to be the one that affirms their identity all the time because then they're always going to need me to affirm their identity instead of going to the Lord.

That's the firstborn mentality of controlling everything and not letting it go. Because if they let it go, then what do they have to bring the fulfillment to them?

That's a negative thing that we can do as leaders. If we're not careful, we pull people towards us instead of pushing them towards the Lord.

Secondly, we don't raise people up because we don't want them to outshine us; we are afraid we will be forgotten. That's a very middle child mentality. To operate in a way where, "If I if I raise up a worship leader that sings better than me, or can move the room better than me, I'll just be forgotten and left in the dust." That's insecurity and not knowing who we are.

Third, we don't operate or move in the gifts of the Spirit because we don't feel qualified or deserving. What happens if we sit at a table, and there's a whole basket of fruit, the fruit of the Spirit? We wait for Him to give them to us instead of taking the fruit and eating or taking the gift and opening it and actually using it.

That comes from not knowing that He loves us. Because He loves us, we can have access to everything.

Fourth, we are afraid of what others will think. We are afraid that we'll look arrogant or that we're going to come across as crazy. We're afraid of what other people are thinking. We don't want to look overbearing if we step out or if we take risks. Even the thought of, "What if I take this risk and I fall on my face?" That comes from the mentality that God won't really catch me if I step out.

Fifth, we become content with being a background person; someone who is afraid to take risks. I understand that there are background people that are meant to serve behind the scenes, which some people prefer. Jesus was not a backseat God; He didn't hide in the shadows. He was in the forefront of changing people's lives. He was in the forefront of loving people and being loud about His love. Whether we serve behind the scenes, we're still called as a people to take risks and be seen by our love.

Here are four things to remember as you continue to walk with the Lord and grow in your identity:

1. You have a history, and this history feeds your confidence. You know He is going to back you; you have a history with God. Nobody can take away your history. Nobody can take away the things that you have in your heart and that He's spoken

to you. He's proven Himself and the application for this is to build stones of remembrance.

Always be journaling. I write songs as stones of remembrance. I can always go back and listen to what God did when I recorded a song. If you paint, you can paint a picture of what God did, put it on your wall, and it can be the declaration of what God did in your life. Or maybe you can make a pot or build a practical stone of remembrance that you can look back at and see the faithfulness of God to remind you that He was faithful.

2. Eat of the fruit and then use the gifts of the Spirit. Then we will show love, joy, peace, patience, kindness, goodness, faithfulness, gentleness, and self-control.

3. Know you hear Him. This is just a reconfirmation that you hear God. That was something that I had to break through in my dark night of the soul season because I was irritated that He was speaking to me in a different way. I questioned whether He was even talking to me at all. When you hear Him, step out and do what He's saying.

4. Fear is not your leader. Believe that you can do anything. Don't go back and forth. Once you jump off the diving board, you can't go back at that point. Jump off the diving board and talk to that person at the gas station or lay hands on them. Give them that word of knowledge. Step out and

do the things that are risky because you can do anything.

Questions for reflection:

How have you seen the effects of your natural birth order in a positive way and/or a negative way? What would change if you could walk as the lastborn of God?

Lesson 20 Small Moves That Have a Big Impact

Chris Mathis

I've been thinking about small moves that have a huge impact. I was reminded in prayer about Moses' mom, weaving a basket that she thought was just for fruits and vegetables, but rather, it was going to be the container that saved her son, Moses, when he was released into a river.

Something that seemed so insignificant, something so mundane and so ordinary, became the container that saved the nation.

Many times, we overlook the day-to-day small things that each of us is entrusted with because we live in a culture that applauds the stage, the lights, the show, and the one who is on the frontlines. But there would not be a Moses had there not been a Moses' mom, who was doing the mundane, normal, day-to-day stuff. That normality was able to save her son and ultimately save a nation.

There are a few other examples that I was thinking about. The woman that gave her last meal to Elijah, in 1 Kings, was something seen as so small, yet it was something so significant. All she had was one jar of oil and some cakes; then she and her son were going to die. She took that small, every day, normal, mundane thing, sowed it, and it caused the multiplication to come into her life.

Another example is David, who was being faithful in the mundane to follow his father's orders by delivering lunch to his brothers on the battlefield. He was delivering meals, and he found himself in the crosshairs of his destiny, doing something so simple, so mundane, such as delivering lunch to his brothers.

What about the young boy who sowed his lunch that over 5000 people ate? Something so mundane—so practical, so simple as him giving his lunch—made such a huge impact as it fed over 5000 people.

These examples are all throughout the Bible. The small moves from humanity that cause heaven's kiss to respond. I want to build off this thought.

We can get so consumed by our culture, enamored by what seems to be great from a stage, or a book that someone writes, or an album someone releases. If we're not careful, we might say we have massive impact in the big things, but we overlook ourselves in the day-to-day simplicity of what God has called us to do.

We get influenced by followers and likes—who's the trending artist, preacher, author, etc.—that we chase those things instead of being faithful with the promises of God and what He's given right before us. We end up overlooking the small things that God has entrusted us with that have the greatest capacity to impact.

So, how do we do focus on the small things?

1. Daily consistency and faithfulness will lead you into the fulfillment of the promises of God for your life. Too

many people are wanting to be discovered in their gift instead of being faithful and consistent in the mundane.

It was a fact that David was anointed. The prophet declared him king, poured oil on his head, and called him out among his family. But David went right back out to the sheep field. He went right back to the mundane, tending his father's sheep, feeding them every day, working in the fields, and working as a farmer. David didn't run right into the battlefield. He didn't skip and gallop his way to the throne.

He was anointed to be king, but he was also going back to his consistency and faithfulness to serve his father. And it was that one normal day his father asked him to bring his brothers' their lunch. That day changed everything for David. But it was daily consistency and faithfulness that led him there.

Ask yourself: am I doing everything I can? Everything that I can do in my craft, my skill, my ministry or my job unto the Lord and am I doing it with excellence?

2. I'm sure we've all heard that it's not about what people do or about what people see you do that makes you successful—it's what you do when nobody's looking. This goes down to the smallest degrees of character.

We often hear that preached in men's conferences. It's not about what you do in public, it's about what you do in private. What are you looking at on your computer when nobody's watching? Let's just dumb that way down for a minute. What do you do when you see a piece of trash? Do you expect someone else to pick it up?

That's the character that I'm talking about. It comes down to what you do when you are not in the public eye, what you do privately when you're all by yourself. If there's an empty coffee cup sitting on the sidewalk, do you pick it up? These things matter to the Lord. When you walk in that, you start to impact others to do the same thing.

I was thinking about my impact as a leader. Jamie Paton and I joke about this often, as Jamie was a senior pastor for several years, and he would come and preach for me, and I'd go and preach for him. We don't do this now, but back then we did quite a bit. Whenever I left town, problems always happened. Jamie used to say, "When the cat's away, the mice play." So cheesy but true.

The marking of your impact as a leader isn't what gets done when you're present. It's what gets done when you're absent. The marking of real leadership is empowering people.

3. I must know and believe that I'm here to change the world in what I do. If I believe it's not yet—if it's going to be one day when I finally reach that stage or one day when I finally write a book—it's not enough.

I must know and believe that I'm here to change the world by what I do in my craft, my skill, my ministry, or my job.

Every social media post has the potential to impact the world. You have no idea that every child who comes through the doors of the church could be the next Billy Graham. You can pray for someone who becomes a millionaire.

I have a friend named Kevin Wallace. He pastors at a church in Chattanooga with about 300 people. There was a kid in his church who was on drugs, and they brought him in. They let him be around the leaders and I think he began cleaning the church and was being mentored. A year or two went by and this kid was delivered from drugs. One day, his dad asked for a meeting with the pastor. He said, "I want to meet with you because my son went through rehab after rehab after rehab. Nothing was able to change his life. So, I want to take you to dinner." After the meal, the parents sat back and asked Kevin, "Tell us your dream." Kevin shared his vision, everything that he wanted to do, especially to start a Bible college and to see the city of Chattanooga, Tennessee, touched by the glory of God.

The man asked, "How much will that cost you?" Kevin said, "I don't know. Maybe ten or twelve million dollars." The father said to his wife, "Honey, break out the chequebook." They cut him a cheque right there, slid it across the table for the exact amount of money. That changed Kevin's church's destiny. It was the faithfulness in the mundane. You never know when God is going to bless your faithfulness.

Questions for reflection:

What small area of your life have you overlooked that has the potential to have great impact? What small things does the Lord want you to do that you are not currently doing?

Around the Table

130

Lesson 21 A Sound Mind

TJ Green

I have been meditating on what it means to have a sound mind.

For God has not given us a spirit of fear, but of power and of love and of a sound mind. 2 Timothy 1:7 NKJV

I've been through about 20 years of full-time ministry, and this is the fourth church that I've been part of.

The first three months of my introduction to ministry was in Sylvan Lake, where the lead pastor got fired after three months, and I was the only person on staff. My introduction into ministry was spiritual warfare, it was about a religious spirit trying to take leaders out.

I've noticed it's not a frontal assault when the enemy attacks. It's usually from multiple angles. He's attacking your finances. He's attacking your health. He's attacking your marriage. He's attacking you from all sides. And it's right when something big is about to go down, when there's a big conference, when there's a big outreach, when there's a big mission of God that is advancing.

As leaders we need to empower people in how to have a sound mind because there will be warfare, there will be seasons of great attack against your mind.

As I was thinking about this verse, in 2 Timothy, I went into the background of what was happening when Paul wrote to Timothy.

This Scripture is at the beginning of the letter. Timothy was a new, young pastor of a new church plant called Ephesus. The church was exploding, it was growing, and it was becoming a threat to the Roman Empire. It was on Nero's radar. Nero's soldiers wanted to capture Timothy, the leader of the church at Ephesus, and give him a brutal, horrible torture and death just as they were doing to other Christians at this time.

We've had persecution in the church, but nothing compared to what the church of Ephesus was going through. They wanted people alive and to light them on fire in public.

The threat to their body and the threat to their lives was in the face of the church every day. They probably heard rumours every week that soldiers were looking for Timothy to kill him.

So, Paul said to Timothy, "God has not given you a spirit of fear." Why?

Timothy was probably thinking about his kids, his family, himself, his church and how they could all be burned to death. The threat was real. Nero's secret police would take special pleasure in killing him in some horrible, barbaric way.

As Timothy was considering this threat against his life, you can easily imagine how he'd have to be dealing with the spirit of fear trying to grab hold of his life.

Paul addressed this right at the beginning of the letter and said, "God has not given you a spirit of fear. He's given you power, love, and a sound mind."

I don't know what you have gone through. I don't know what you're facing right now. The enemy could be trying to intimidate you.

God's saying the same thing to you right now. I love making the Bible personal, like Paul was writing a letter to me and saying, "TJ, God hasn't given you a spirit of fear. He's given you a spirit of power, love, and a sound mind."

I'm going to zero in on that phrase, a 'sound mind'.

Sofronismeo is the Greek word for sound mind and it's a compound word of two different words. One word is very similiar to *Sozo*, which means salvation. The other is *froneo*. *Sozo* means to be saved and delivered. It is suggesting that something is delivered, rescued, revived, salvaged, protected, safe, and secure. The word *sozo* could depict a person who was on the verge of death, but who was revived, resuscitated, and had new life breathed back in.

Froneo carries the idea of a person's intelligence, their total frame of thinking, including the rationale, their logic and their emotions. The word *froneo* refers to every part of the human mind, including the process that we engage in making the mind function and coming to conclusions.

When you combine these two words together, you can translate the Scripture and it adds to the definition, perhaps like this:

God has not given you a spirit of fear, but of power and of love. He has given you a mind that has been delivered, rescued, revived, salvaged, and protected. He has brought you into a place of safety and security in your thinking, so that it's no longer affected by illogical, unfounded, and absurd fears or thoughts.

That's the mind that God has given you. As leaders, I saw a picture of the weapons of our warfare. God gives you the sword of the spirit, the belt of truth, and the breastplate of righteousness. I've seen this in the spirit several times. It's like God was putting helmets on people. And it's the helmet of *sozo*. It's the helmet of nothing missing, nothing broken, total perfect peace, total perfect wholeness in your thinking, in your heart, and in your emotions. He puts that helmet on your heads.

You have the ability to think like that. You can think as if you have the mind of Christ. God has given you the mind of Christ. You can think like God thinks. Sometimes, I see this in meetings where God is doing mental health miracles, and He's rewiring the way people are thinking.

When Saul was trying to put his helmet on David, it didn't fit his way of thinking, his way of doing warfare. It wasn't working and David rejected the armour. Why? Because he was already armoured in the secret place. He'd already been singing songs; he had already sung his way into victory before he got to the battlefield. That's why when he showed up, he was already thinking a different way. "Who is this Philistine, and why are we allowing him to talk this way?"

Because David was thinking a different way, he had already won the battle in his mind and his heart. He had been in the secret place in times of increased warfare and intimacy with God, so he could start thinking like God.

If you're dealing with intense warfare, lock yourself in the secret place; go hide in the caves. When you have that helmet of salvation, the enemy will still try to attack you with thoughts, but those fiery darts will bounce off; they won't stick. You'll recognize, "That's not my thought. That's the enemy. That's not victorious thinking, that's carnal thinking. That's natural thinking. And I've got a supernatural mind. God has given me the helmet of salvation."

God's thought stabilized David and gave him courage. Sometimes you need to remind yourselves of the truth that is always a superior reality of the circumstances that you might be in. There is a truth that is superior to the facts of the situations that you find yourselves in. As you grow in ministry, there will be increased warfare, and things that maybe early on, you wouldn't have been able to handle, you grow to be able to handle.

With the increased warfare that you find yourselves in, say five or ten years from now, it's going to be like water off a duck's back. You will realize you've been through this before, and things that are stressing you out right now won't anymore.

God is going to grow you in authority, and those things aren't going to stress you out anymore. A lot of people don't know what you're going through, but it doesn't matter, you've got a sound mind. It is only going to get better in the future as you lean into Him.

Questions for Reflection:

How has God changed your mind? Has there been a moment or maybe a testimony when the Word of God protected your mind in the face of real spiritual warfare?

Lesson 22 Legacy

Tracy Belford

I was pondering, how do we create legacy?

Legacy, according to the dictionary, has two definitions. One is an amount of money or property left to someone in a will. The second definition is the long-lasting impact of particular events, actions, etc., that took place in the past or of a person's life.

The long-lasting impact of particular events is what I'm talking about. When my kids were young, I would ask myself, "What am I doing of eternal consequence?"

When you are raising kids, it's hard. You feel like you are just wiping poopy bums all day long, and doing a mountain of laundry, and wondering how it is important.

At some point, I realized, it was incredibly important. All of that was legacy. My kids saw the attitude in which I served them. They saw the attitude in which I washed the dishes. They saw how I served my husband. All those things create legacy.

Even the littlest, tiniest things that you think are inconsequential when you're parenting cause legacy. But it took me a while to wrap my head around that—that all these things that I thought were totally unimportant had eternal consequence and were not just temporal.

Now, in this season of my life, where my kids are all doing their own adult things, I started asking again, "What am I doing that has eternal consequences?"

I felt like in the grand scheme of things, most of what I do now doesn't have eternal consequences, but then upon further reflection, I find that it does.

I have way more one-time contacts with people now; often I pray for somebody at the altar and never see them again. In my head, I don't view that as highly important because I don't see the outcome. Then I started shifting my perspective and realizing that when I laid hands on them, it radically changed their life, even if I don't see that outcome with my eyes.

It became important for me to start shifting my view to see the eternal consequence to what my actions are, knowing that a right word at the right time can change everything for somebody.

So how do we create legacy? How do we create long-lasting impact?

The first way I think we do it is that we must be intentional. In the first definition of legacy, about inheriting money or property that's left to someone in a will, you don't get left something in a will unless the deceased person earned the money. Somone worked hard for it, or it wouldn't exist.

If there's no will, then the money is not left to you. The planning of writing a will itself creates legacy. So, to have a legacy, you must be intentional. You must have a plan and a purpose to be able to create legacy.

A good person leaves an inheritance for their children's children, but a sinner's wealth is stored up for the righteous. Proverbs 13:22a NIV

There are a lot of other verses that imply legacy, like the Old Testament concept of birthright. When they laid hands on their firstborn son, they were giving legacy. When they talked about the God of Abraham, Isaac, and Jacob, they were talking about legacy. Even the fact that the Israelites knew their genealogies from Adam all the way down is legacy.

We have to consider: what kind of legacy are we trying to leave? Is it about wealth? Is it about scriptural knowledge? Is it about faith or miracles or celebrations? What is the legacy we're trying to leave? Without intentionality, we never even decide what we want to leave.

The second step would be a plan of action. If my goal is a legacy of faith, I need to walk in faith. I need to have opportunities to do it and then take risks. I couldn't just leave a legacy of faith without the plan of action.

The third step would be that I'd have to succeed in taking those risks or at least have the target of my inheritance be around to observe me doing it, or to leave them a record of some sort. If the risks weren't witnessed or recorded, no one would know.

When we think about the revivals of the past, how do we know about them? They were written down. They were recorded somehow, or there were people who lived to see them who continued to talk about them. I think of the

Welsh Revival, Aimee Semple McPherson, or even John Wimber. We can only access an inheritance if we know about it.

I wonder how many other revivals have happened that weren't recorded, and we've lost the history. We just don't know. Why did the Bible get written as a record, as a testament, to what happened? If we didn't have the written word of God, it would be much harder for us to understand His heart. This is all legacy.

For us to leave a legacy, we need to consider what kind of legacy we want to leave, make a plan of action, and then step out and take risks to complete our legacy.

Questions for reflection:

What is your personal legacy? How does the Lord want you to be more intentional in creating legacy? What kind of risks do you need to take to create the legacy you desire?

Lesson 23 Marriage

Des Belford

Tracy and I have walked with people in various stages of their marriages whether the couples are deciding to get married, become engaged, or have been married for a little while or a long time.

Through all my experience, there are certain things that are important, and this isn't a comprehensive list, but I want to highlight some of the important points.

The church has gotten away from some of its basic fundamental precepts. We've outsourced some areas, and we don't talk as readily or as freely about some of these things, either because it became taboo, or because we've had bad traditions, teaching, or theology. I feel it is very important we talk about these things amongst ourselves as leaders, but also that we teach our church body and our families about them.

Covenant is the first and foremost thing. It usually is the first thing that blows people's minds because they don't have an understanding of covenant. When they say their vows, they promise to have and to hold, but they don't really understand what that means.

Marriage starts before you're even married. In the old Jewish customs, the father and husband-to-be would meet. The prospective groom was arranged. There would be a negotiation of terms of covenant, and the dowry would be paid.

Back then, it would be very common for spouses at that point to actually call each other husband or wife. Mary was betrothed to Joseph, and she would have called him her husband, once the betrothal happened, even though they hadn't been intimate yet.

Then the father and the groom would part, and the groom would start building a house and preparing it, making sure it was set up. Once the father was satisfied with the groom's growth and the house that was built, he would tell the groom to come get his bride. There was a big shindig and a feast. There was the wedding, which was a multiple day celebration.

When I talk about covenant, I ask people, "What does it mean and what do you bring to the table?"

A lot of people don't think about what they're bringing into the covenant, both positive and negative.

A marriage covenant is when you enter into a legal spiritual agreement with your spouse and God, with conditions, vows, and roles.

It is important to understand that a covenant is how the culture of your marriage will unfold from the foundation of your relationship to the later years of your marriage. It also sets the foundation for future generations.

It's also important to know that what you bring into this covenant, good or bad, will affect your covenant, such as porn, addictions, unresolved trauma, past marriages, soul ties, blessings, and inheritance.

You must enter into a marriage with clean hands and a pure heart in order to start your marriage on the right path.

Often, we see couples that struggle with intimacy, but there was usually an intimacy issue pre-marriage that wasn't dealt with. If it gets dealt with before the covenant, it is much easier. It is far more beneficial to do the heart-work before you're married than after.

Another important area is what love is and isn't. Love is a choice. Love is work. Marriage is work. Tracy and I have been married for 24 years. It takes a lot of work. We have to choose each other daily.

Love takes action, it takes work, and it takes premeditation. One of the phrases I use is 'to be a pursuer and a pursued'. Being a pursuer means being intentional. It doesn't mean always buying flowers, but it means making sure that your spouse is at the forefront of your mind.

Do you have their heart? Do they have your heart? In communication, before you open your mouth, do you have their heart? Are you pursuing connection? Are you pursuing togetherness? Are you pursuing intimacy and vulnerability? Love is holding their heart and preferring one another in a way that is beneficial to not just you but to them.

My favorite topic, which the church sucks at talking about, is sex and purity. Sex is a good thing. But sex is not the goal. Intimacy is the goal. We need to understand that sex is a byproduct of intimacy. If we're preferring one another, meeting their love language, laying our life down, and pursuing the goal of connection and restoration, being one flesh, then sex is going to happen.

Often people ask, what in sex is healthy, and what is not? This goes back to the whole idea of what you bring into your covenant.

If you've got a porn addiction, you may be bringing in unrealistic expectations of what sex is, which then means you are unfulfilled, and the spouse leaves diminished and violated. The church doesn't need to tell you what is healthy for your marriage. Your spouse does. If they feel diminished or violated in any way, then that act is obviously not healthy.

If communication is there, if you are talking about what you want and need, if intimacy is there, sex will happen.

If you're not having sex in your marriage, you have to ask yourself some questions. Have you been vulnerable with your spouse? Are you checking the boxes of connection? Are you doing the things that helps build healthy sexual culture in your life? Are you communicating?

Another topic is building a marriage of empowerment. One of my favorite scriptures regarding marriage is:

Who can find a virtuous and capable wife? She is more precious than rubies. Her husband can trust her, and she will greatly enrich his life. She brings him good, not harm, all the days of her life. She finds wool and flax and busily spins it. She is like a merchant's ship, bringing her food from afar. She gets up before dawn to prepare breakfast for her household and plan the day's work for her servant girls. She goes to inspect a field and buys it; with her earnings she plants a vineyard. She is energetic and strong, a hard worker. She makes sure her dealings are profitable; her lamp burns late into the night. Her hands are busy spinning thread, her fingers twisting fiber. She extends a helping hand to the poor and opens her arms to the needy. She has no fear of winter for her household, for everyone has warm clothes. She makes her own bedspreads. She dresses in fine linen and purple gowns. Her husband is well known at the city gates, where he sits with the other civic leaders. She makes belted linen garments and sashes to sell to the merchants. She is clothed with strength and dignity, and she laughs without fear of the future. When she speaks, her words are wise, and she gives instructions with kindness. She carefully watches everything in her household and suffers nothing from laziness. Her children stand and bless her. Her husband praises her: There are many virtuous and capable women in the world, but you surpass them all! Proverbs 31:10-29 NLT

Do you trust your wife or husband to buy a field? Meaning do they have the freedom to make a mistake and grow? And are you going to be their biggest champion? Or are you going to be their biggest hindrance?

For instance, Tracy needed a new car; she had requirements, like a backup camera and a heated steering wheel. I had different requirements, like 4-wheel drive. I felt the Lord saying, "Do you trust her? Do you trust her to do this process?" I trusted her, and I needed to communicate that to her, and empower her to make the choice, knowing that she would care about both our requirements, and also knowing that it would be ok if she made a wrong choice. I communicated that to her and empowered her to choose the car.

A lot of heart conditions, especially when you live in survival or self-preservation, don't allow you to empower your spouse. You don't want to empower your spouse because that empowerment has a direct tie to your heart.

If they don't do it the way that you would, does it make it the wrong choice? Or is it ok for them to choose differently than you would, as long as they are holding both your hearts? What if they make a mistake?

When your spouse is not feeling empowered, you are not living in connection. It goes back to submitting and investing your life. (Submitting in the context of preferring one another and holding each other's heart.)

When you get married, you need to come to a place of intimacy and vulnerability together, and connection, so that no matter what you do, you're a team. You're in this together and that's the end goal: to be empowered in such a way that life is good and that everybody's heart is connected.

A key topic of contention is family relations, or as I call them, in-laws and outlaws. Extended family dynamics can be challenging.

Individually, you both grew up in a culture of a home. Your spouse's family had a standard and your family had a standard, and when you get married, you are trying to merge those standards together. Sometimes, especially in the early years, that can be really challenging because of different cultures.

"This is how we did things and so, that's not how you do things." "Well, your mom was wrong." "We eat meals like this." "We put the toilet paper this way."

This is why it's important to talk about what the culture of your home is going to be before you get married. When you are laying the foundation of the culture in your home, you have to ask yourself questions. What is the standard? What is Jesus' standard of your home? What culture do you want?

It's the understanding of why those things were happening in our families of origin. And when you understand, you can have grace. When you have grace, you can develop into a healthy family.

People who go through divorce are shattered. They are broken. We were designed to be knit together. (I am not saying that God cannot restore those who divorce. I am saying it is a painful process.) I believe all marriages can be restored. It doesn't mean it's without hard work and forgiveness. But if you think about it like this, you are better together.

If you want a good picture of what breaking covenant looks like, I want you to imagine a cold grilled cheese sandwich, and I want you to try to separate that sandwich without breaking the bread. You can't. You will destroy the sandwich. That is the nature of covenant.

Tracy and I are completely different people. I am the person who will jump out of the plane before I think about grabbing a parachute. She's the one who grabs the parachute and comes out after me. I'm the kite, she's the string. We are one flesh.

It's important to learn to celebrate your differences and to see that they're not weaknesses, but merely differences. It's important to understand your strengths and your differences so that you can help make them work for your marriage. That builds the bond of togetherness and understanding, which also builds connection.

It's deciding, 'we are better together', and staying together is the goal. A whole person is better than a fractured person. So do the things that matter. Prefer and hold your spouse's heart.

Every marriage is unique because every culture of marriage is unique. All marriages take work and effort, but they have the potential to be life giving, whole, happy relationships that bless the Kingdom of God. What I have shared here is not the manual—it's a Cole's notes, short version of some helpful areas for marriage.

Questions for reflection:

How are you preparing yourself to be a good partner? How are you pursuing intimacy with your spouse? What's the culture of your home?

Lesson 24 The Busyness of Life

Chris Frost

I've been talking to a group of people who have been feeling overwhelmed. Recently, I picked up a book by Patrick Lencioni. I love the way he writes because the first part of the book is a fable, a story that you can identify with, and the last part is practical, how you apply it. His book is called *Three Big Questions For a Frantic Family*, and as I started to read it, it made me laugh.

The conversations in this book are the conversations that my wife, Dominique, and I have. Patrick writes about how at night he and his wife are brushing their teeth, and she says, "Don't forget tomorrow, we have parent teacher interviews, and the day after, there's hockey practice and swimming, and then we have to go here and go there." Then Patrick stops and says, "Listen, we just have to stop committing to so many things." And his wife says, "Great, what are we going to stop committing to?" And Patrick replies, "I don't know," and then they carry on. This resonates with me.

The thief comes only to steal and kill and destroy; I have come that they may have life and have it to the full. John 10:10 NIV

If it feels like it's stealing life, then it's probably not from the Lord.

The LORD's blessing brings wealth, and he adds no trouble to it. Proverbs 10:22 NHEB

To me, if God is bringing this blessing into your life, there shouldn't be any trouble with it; it shouldn't cause stress.

After reading this book, first I asked myself what makes my family unique?

The human body has many parts, but the many parts make up one whole body. So it is with the body of Christ. Some of us are Jews, some are Gentiles, some are slaves, and some are free. But we have all been baptized into one body by one Spirit, and we all share the same Spirit. Yes, the body has many different parts, not just one part. 1 Corinthians 12:12-14 NLT

This idea of my family's uniqueness gives vision for my family, being intentional about what makes us unique and what God has called us to. Finding our uniqueness helps define where we are going. There's no right answer; the answer is unique, just like our families are.

Second, what is my family's story? What is my family's biggest priority? What is the core value that we're all going to rally around? For instance, the one that they wrote about in the book was core family time; that's what they were after. Your family's priorities help make decisions and direct where you go.

Where there is no revelation, people cast off restraint; but blessed is the one who heeds wisdom's instruction. Proverbs 29:18 NIV

In those days Israel had no king; everyone did as they saw fit. Judges 21:25 NIV

When there is no vision, people just do whatever they want. It's the same thing in your family.

As a family, when everything is important, suddenly, nothing becomes important. We get thrown around by every urgent thing. When there is a vision, when I know my family's biggest priority, then we can all rally around that, and we can all be going in the same direction as a family.

Third, how can my family use these answers? How can we use the answers to these questions today, next week, and next year, so it helps us set those priorities?

This book and this topic resonate with me because in organizations and churches, we set values, we set priorities, and we have a vision. For example, The Summit Church exists to influence the city of Edmonton, the province of Alberta, and the nation of Canada with the spirit of revival. We also have core values: family, devotion, revival, and hope.

It sounds weird to have a vision statement and core values as a family. The reason we don't is because we're not going to get fired from our family. No one's going to kick us out. No one's going to say, "Hey, you haven't been adhering to our vision. Dinner was late three days in a row. So sorry, I'm going to find someone else to marry." That's not what we do. There's unconditional love in our families.

By being intentional, we can go after those things that really matter, as opposed to letting life just happen to us.

Questions for reflection:

Do you have clearly articulated values or things that make you unique as a family? If so, what are they? How are you dealing with the busyness of life?

Lesson 25 Come as a Child

Nikki Mathis

Beloved identity is the revelation—it's the foundation that changes everything in the way that we live our lives with the Lord and how we can access things in the spirit.

We should be able to access these revelations our whole lives, but when we're trying to heal from striving, the works mentality hinders us from being able to access the fullness that the spirit realm has available to us.

I really believe that this principle, this key of the Kingdom, is the reason for that. It is the childlike faith where those who come like a child will enter the Kingdom of heaven. And unless we come like a child and unless we have that position of our heart to be childlike, we will not enter the Kingdom of heaven.

The Kingdom of heaven is not a place that we go when we die. It's not just about heaven. It's the Kingdom realm, here on Earth that we can have access to, that is tangible. It's where we pull the supernatural out of the unseen into our tangible world that brings healing to people and brings the manifestation of Christ here on Earth.

I want to talk about the childlike faith revelation and challenge us to go deeper. I feel like it is the foundation of why beloved identity changes everything. It is because it forces us to stop being professional Christians and go back to just being like a child; a child that's resting and knowing he's loved.

At that time the disciples came to ask Jesus, "Who is considered to be the greatest in heaven's kingdom realm?" Jesus called a little one to his side and said to them, "Learn this well: Unless you dramatically change your way of thinking and become teachable like a little child, you will never be able to enter in. Whoever continually humbles himself to become like this little child is the greatest one in heaven's kingdom realm. Matthew 18:1-4 TPT

In the footnotes, a child is defined as a toddler, and also, the word that Jesus uses in Aramaic is *talitha*, which comes from the word for wounded lamb. Those hearing Jesus would have heard both meanings, a little child or a lamb.

We could change our way of thinking and come like children, ones who continually humble themselves. It means to see ourselves as unimportant in our own eyes. When I read this, I thought, "Well, we're trying to not look at ourselves and see the worst that we have. We want to believe in beloved identity, we want to know that we're valuable, but does that mean we see ourselves as a toddler?"

It's a double-sided coin. On one side, I don't want to think higher of myself than I should, but on the other side, I want to know my worth and my value and walk in the confidence of what God's put in me.

Toddlers are not sitting there thinking about all the ways that they're going to benefit the world, or how amazing they are, or about the worth they carry. All they're thinking about is that they just want to be with their father, and they want to have fun with him. To become like a little child is to be the greatest one in the Kingdom of heaven's realm.

Jesus said, "Let the little children come to me, and do not hinder them, for the kingdom of heaven belongs to such as these." Matthew 19:14 NIV

In this verse, Jesus overheard people wanting to bring the kids to Him so He could bless them. And the disciples didn't want to bother Him.

This is important. I know that we really value children, and we understand their worth and their role, but Jesus wanted them close. Jesus overheard the disciples and said, "I want little children to come to me." Heaven's Kingdom realm is composed of beloved ones like these.

Listen to this truth. No one will enter the Kingdom realm of heaven unless he becomes like one of these. Then Jesus laid his hands on each one of them and went on His way.

We as adults must change our mindset. We need to change the way we think, which is repentance; we need to repent, to change the way that we've been viewing ourselves. That's how we have access to the Kingdom.

An adult mindset would allow the responsibilities to produce a lack of trust in both God and people. The Kingdom child mindset is that people just believe anything we tell them. They just believe whatever Jesus says to be true.

Whereas an adult, when we've been let down and when we've had situations that didn't pan out the way we were hoping, starts to build a mentality where we can't trust.

An adult life mindset would be ambition to build business and ministry and make money. It's what we have on our minds because we're adults. We make money and provide, but the Kingdom child mindset is that our only ambition is to be with our parents. It's really all we care about.

An adult life mindset is to worry about health, family, and money. Children don't worry about what clothes they will wear, and they don't even care if their clothes match.

In an adult life mindset, accomplishments produce pride. In a Kingdom child mindset, we have humility, and we don't think highly of ourselves. Or even if we accomplish something, we move on right away. We don't let our heads get big.

An adult life mindset has a hard time disconnecting from earthly things, whereas children's mindsets are quick to disengage from earthly things.

Adults hold onto their right to be offended or withhold forgiveness, whereas children are so quick to forgive and forget and move forward without walls. They're so quick to forgive and to look past all our flaws and all the things that we do wrong, even as their parents.

If we can repent and come to the Lord like little children again, it makes it so much easier for us to quickly forgive each other and move forward without walls.

Children are completely helpless. We have to take care of them. An adult life mindset depends on their business or their job to feed the children.

In essence, our Father just wants to be with us. He wants our devotion to be worry-free and performance-free. He wants us to sit and be like a child with Him.

Questions for reflection:

What childlike characteristic have you lost because of maturity? How would having that characteristic benefit your beloved identity walk with God?

Around the Table

Lesson 26 Rejection & Abandonment

Tracy Belford

I spend a lot of time doing inner healing and deliverance ministry, and I have found a common thread that every person who comes in struggles with. I've recognized over time that this is a pattern, that these two things are a human issue. Everybody has them. It's common to all of us. For some people, they are small issues, but for other people, they're much bigger issues, depending on what their life experience has been. I've come to understand that none of us escape from life without having to deal with these two problems.

Many people allow these issues to become their identity, and to form belief systems about them. They say, "This happened, and therefore I'm expecting more of this."

The two things that I see in all people are rejection and abandonment. We all struggle with them to some degree or another. I spent a lot of time dealing with these issues with people when we're doing inner healing and deliverance because they seem to be some of the biggest roots.

I was thinking about the spiritual truth that says that we press into the opposite spirit. What is the opposite of rejection and abandonment? How can we partner with the Lord to heal people? How can we lift them up out of where they're at?

The answer to the first problem is easy. The opposite of rejection is acceptance. That means that when we're ministering in a way that brings healing, we show a person that we accept them. Accepting them as a person is hugely important. We don't accept their sin, but we accept who they are. We show acceptance by body language, tone, and the words we use. That's how we show we accept somebody. We tell people that we accept them for who they are, just like Jesus. There's no question about that. He doesn't require us to clean up our life to accept us, He just accepts us. This is a facet of beloved identity. There's nothing we must do to be accepted by Jesus. It's just automatic.

What's the opposite of abandonment? I tried to nail it down and I couldn't. I couldn't express what the exact opposite word for abandonment was. So, how do we press into the opposite spirit if we don't even know what it is?

After not hearing an answer from Jesus, I googled it. The first thing that came up as the opposite of abandonment was adoption. I did not see that coming. I was shocked. I suddenly looked at all the Scriptures in the Bible about adoption and saw them very differently. I thought to myself that those who have adopted children probably know this much better than the rest of us.

I'm going to take you through some of those Scriptures.

God sent him to buy freedom for us who were slaves to the law, so that he could adopt us as his very own children. And because we are his children, God has sent the Spirit of his Son into our hearts, prompting us to call out, "Abba, Father." Now you are no longer a slave but God's own child. And since you are his child, God has made you his heir. Galatians 4:5-7 NLT

God decided in advance to adopt us into his own family by bringing us to himself through Jesus Christ. This is what he wanted to do, and it gave him great pleasure. Ephesians 1:5 NLT

God decided in advance, and He predestined to take us out of abandonment into adoption as sons. That hits differently.

So you have not received a spirit that makes you fearful slaves. Instead, you received God's Spirit when he adopted you as his own children. Now we call him, "Abba, Father." Romans 8:15 NLT

In other words, 'For you did not receive the spirit of slavery and abandonment, to fall back into fear, but you've received the Spirit of adoption.'

And we believers also groan, even though we have the Holy Spirit within us as a foretaste of future glory, for we long for our bodies to be released from sin and suffering. We, too, wait with eager hope for the day when God will give us our full rights as his adopted children, including the new bodies he has promised us. Romans 8:23 NLT

To rephrase part of this, 'As we wait eagerly for adoption as sons and daughters, the redemption of our bodies from abandonment....'

All of these things hit me differently because adoption hasn't ever really meant anything to me. I'm not adopted, and I don't have any adopted children, so I never really understood the adoption Scriptures.

In light of this, most of us haven't experienced complete abandonment. Most of us are orphans, to some degree, but not completely orphaned. My dad died but I still had my mom. We had measures of abandonment. Our parents didn't disown us and walk away leaving us as orphans. We see abandonment in a different light. We were abandoned in part but not in whole. But we have been abandoned repeatedly and that reinforces the belief.

What happens if we take God at His Word and apply adoption to every place that we've been abandoned? This is why the spirit of adoption is so powerful. I had to question: why did the Lord put in that word the way He did? Why did He utilize adoption in different places in Scripture? Why was adoption so important to Him?

It's because this is the key. It's a common issue to all mankind that we need adoption so that we no longer feel abandoned. Adoption is permanent. It's legal. It has lifetime and inheritance ramifications.

After I googled and found the answer that the opposite of abandonment is adoption, I found another answer. It was specifically about the opposite of abandonment issues. It said the opposite of abandonment is togetherness. Togetherness often brings a sense of security that is appealing for those dealing with abandonment issues.

Abandonment erodes our self-esteem and self-worth, hence causing us to seek security elsewhere.

God, knowing how He created us and how the issues of rejection and abandonment would be common to all mankind, addressed these issues in His Word.

Questions for reflection:

How have God's acceptance and adoption changed you? How can you use these spiritual truths to minister to others?

Around the Table

Lesson 27 Sight vs Vision

Paulina Guinez

Never doubt God's mighty power to work in you and accomplish all this. He will achieve infinitely more than your greatest request, your most unbelievable dream, and exceed your wildest imagination! He will outdo them all, for his miraculous power constantly energizes you. Ephesians 3:20 TPT

Personally, a word God has spoken over me and has consistently brought up is to have higher expectations and believe for more.

The Lord has been talking to me about vision and purpose, the *why* behind why we do what we do, who I am, and why sight is not good enough when wanting to walk in the fullness of what God has for me.

He showed me that there is a difference between sight and vision. Sight is physical, it is what's right in front of us, whereas vision is mental. The organs of sight are the eyes whereas the organs of vision are the heart and the mind. Sight is bound by time and distance. Vision is bound by the imagination; it is creative and outside of the box of sight. Vision includes what has not been seen or done before. Sight may allow a person to witness an event, but vision helps the person understand the significance of that event and draw interpretations. The two are harmonious and are very important in our everyday lives.

People are often trapped solely in sight, what is right in front of them, which is the bare minimum for survival, and they forget their vision, which is their imagination, creating expectation and dreaming with the Lord.

Sometimes, we walk through life letting life just happen instead of partnering with the Lord and creating a life filled with dreams, purpose, and vision. Everyone has sight and can see, but not everyone has vision.

Visionaries don't just sit in the day-to-day—they create a dream, partner with faith, and look past sight. There is a witty invention waiting to be made; there is a never-before-created business model ready to be built, and there is a miracle waiting to be released!

Where there is no vision, the people perish: but he that keepeth the law, happy is he. Proverbs 29:19 KJV

Some synonyms for vision are dream, foresight, imagination, outlook, understanding, discernment for knowledge, intuition, and awareness.

Some antonyms for vision are blindness, sightlessness, non-discerning, and not building for the future.

There is a great deal of difference between sight and vision, if only we will see it.

Questions for reflection:

Are you dreaming and creating with the Lord? Are you partnering with vision with the Lord? What hinders your vision?

Lesson 28 God as Father

Rebekah Ryzuk

For almost a year, I've started my day by just saying, "Good morning, God, good morning, Holy Spirit, good morning, Jesus." It helped to set my heart in the right direction each day and become intentionally aware of their presence in my life.

Recently, I started as I normally do, "Good morning God," and immediately I heard a question pop up in my heart. "Why do you always call me God and not Father or Dad?"

After wrestling through my thoughts and searching my heart, I concluded that if I was really honest with myself, it had nothing to do with my relationship with my dad. Actually, it was a result of watching the way it seemed that God treated my dad as a pastor and not believing that God was a good father for treating him that way.

As a pastor's kid, I grew up watching my dad pour his entire life out for God. Our church brought my dad in as the pastor when it was deeply in debt. From my perspective, our family was pushed into absolute financial chaos for the next decade as a result of pastoring. My dad didn't get a salary for years, money always seemed to be tight, and I knew that the lack was stressful on our family.

As a family with many kids, we lived out of town, raised goats, and had a massive garden to help offset the grocery bills. I went through my childhood watching God provide miracle after miracle. People would randomly come by with groceries, clothes, toys, and whatever else we needed. I knew without a doubt that God was a provider. You might assume that I'd have such an appreciation for the provision, and I did, but I also believed deeply that He was a last minute, when you're 'about to die', provider of just barely enough to get by.

We saw miracle after miracle, but I wasn't thankful for those. I wanted less stress, fresh new clothes, the latest toys, and a family vacation! I did not appreciate this last-minute miracle God.

I still have the journal entry in which I accused God of not caring when I was about 12 years old. I wrote, "If this is the way you treat your servants, your kids, I don't want anything to do with it. It's not fair, it's not okay."

From my perspective, the way God treated my dad was abusive. I felt my dad worked hard to serve God, but God couldn't be bothered to give him enough blessing to take a little stress off the grocery bill and get his kids new clothes. He provided just enough to keep us coming back, but not enough to fulfill any sort of promise.

We repeatedly had people come through our church who would give prophecies about abundance and no more lack, quoting so many Bible verses full of promise. But to my young perspective, all these promises in the Bible seemed like a carrot dangling just out of reach to keep us serving God. It seemed rather cruel.

I concluded that I didn't think of God as a dad because I couldn't imagine a dad being so mean to his kids. To call

Him "God" kept Him at a safe distance; it avoided having to define my relationship with Him as a father.

In my heart I asked, "God, how could you do that to my dad?" My own heart came up with all the good church kid answers, but I couldn't accept any of them. The words sounded good but didn't touch the pain deep in my heart. It took a couple of weeks before my own internal wrestling match between the hurt and the good "Christian" answers quieted down enough for me to hear His answer.

As I drove to work one morning, I suddenly heard a voice in my spirit that broke through and completely interrupted my thoughts. It was a voice that I hadn't heard before, and I don't even know how to describe it, but it was a deeper tone than what I normally hear in my heart. "Can you hear Me now?" Immediately, I knew that this was the voice of Father God.

I answered, "Yeah, I can! I can hear You."

He said, "When you were young, your parents walked through things that you couldn't understand. I took them through these things because your generation needed to know how to believe in Me for those miracles. I wanted the miracles to be so normal for you that you'd never doubt that I would come though."

As God spoke to me, it brought such healing to my heart. He was right, I always knew that God would provide; there was never a question about it. It was normal for us to see miracles of provision. I had completely taken it for granted, and I had forgotten to be thankful for what had become so common.

In that same conversation, I heard God ask, "What do you want? How can I show you that I'm a good dad?"

I asked what popped into my mind, "I want to bring my kids to the waterpark and just have a fun day like everyone else gets to! I don't want them to miss out because we don't have the money! That's what I want! If you were a good dad, you'd want your kids to have fun together."

He said, "Then book the time and the tickets."

Immediately, my mind began to race. "That's not wise because we are drowning in debt. I can't. It would be fun but no, I can't do that!" I almost wrote off the entire idea but decided to talk to my husband and ask him. I was 99% sure he wouldn't agree and the whole thing would be closed. However, after about 3 weeks of consideration, my husband said, "Okay, if you are sure God spoke to you, then we'll do it."

We booked the tickets. In fact, when we found a good deal on the tickets, I decided to push the line a little further and booked to bring another family with us. Within about five days, an unexpected government credit came into our account that was almost the exact amount that I spent on the waterpark tickets for us all!

At that moment, I realized that God really cared. He cared about my family, He cared about fun, and He cared about the things we wanted even if we didn't "need" them. Mostly, He cared about reaching my heart and healing some deep hurt from the past so I could receive Him as my Father.

I didn't realize that the characteristic of God as 'Dad' or 'Father' was blocked off in my life because I wouldn't accept it due to past hurt. This was a real revelation for me. I believe that I created a wall that kept myself from fully experiencing the Father's love because I couldn't embrace Him as Father. He loved past that wall and reached me—like a good Father.

Questions for reflection:

What characteristic or name of God do you have the hardest time embracing? Was that caused by something in your past?

Around the Table

Lesson 29 Jesus Style Leadership

TJ Green

I have been studying Jesus' style of leadership, and I feel convicted. My heart has been broken where I see the church has failed, and where I've failed.

Jacob and John, sons of Zebedee, approached Jesus and said, "Teacher, will you do us a favor?" "What is it?" he asked, "We want to sit next to you when you come into your glory," they said, "one at your right hand and the other at your left." Jesus replied, "You don't have a clue what you're asking for! Are you prepared to drink from the cup of suffering that I am about to drink? And are you able to endure the baptism into death that I am about to experience?" They replied, "Yes, we are able." Jesus said to them, "You will certainly drink from the cup of my sufferings and be immersed into my death, but to have you sit in the position of highest honor is not mine to decide. It is reserved for those especially prepared to have it."

Now the other ten disciples overheard this, and they became angry and began to criticize Jacob and John. Jesus gathered them all together and said to them, "Those recognized as rulers of the people and those who are in top leadership positions rule oppressively over their subjects, but this is not the example you are to follow. You are to lead by a different model. If you want to be the greatest, then live as one called to serve others. The path to promotion comes by having the heart of a bond-slave who serves everyone. For even the Son of Man did not come expecting to be served by everyone, but to serve everyone, and to give his life as the ransom price for the salvation of many." Mark 10:35-45 TPT

Desiring to be the greatest and have influence is not a bad thing. God put that in us. But Jesus essentially said, 'There's a way to get there. I have to be a bondservant; you have to be a servant of all.' That's a hard thing. To be a leader you have to be a servant of all.

Even the Son of Man did not come to be served by everyone, but to serve everyone and to give His life as the ransom price for the salvation of many.

When I was with Brian Simmons, he was talking about going to churches where there have been leaders who have insulated themselves with people who are so loyal to the church and loyal to them that they couldn't even be questioned. They also couldn't be accessed. Brian said it was gross. It reminded him of the mafia, because they couldn't be questioned and couldn't be wrong. But they were good at crowd control. Their church was really good at handling people.

Kenneth Hagan has often said, "Don't believe everything I preach. You have to go and test everything that I'm saying." Paul said, "Follow me as I follow Jesus." We must follow Jesus.

The letters that we read in the Bible, Paul took to the other disciples and said, "Am I hearing God?" He submitted to them and even corrected and reviewed the other leaders.

I think healthy, confident leaders welcome the sifting of the Holy Spirit. If you're ever offended and you're in a leadership position, and you're questioned in that leadership position, that could be insecurity or pride rearing its head in your life.

I believe healthy leaders are not above reproach, because they are consistently testing their own heart. They welcome times of testing, times of question. In a healthy way, not in an aggressive way, they're like, "Bring it on. I have nothing to hide. My heart is fully exposed." They ask the heart of God to see if there are any selfish motives, any pride, any compromise in them.

One of the things I learned from Pastor Peter Nash was to test the words that come from your enemies and your critics. Weigh them. Don't dismiss them but instead ask if there is any reason for the attack. They might not have your best interests in mind. They might want to tear you down. They might legitimately be your enemies, and slander you, but is there any merit in anything they say?

An interesting moment of Jesus' model of leadership was when He was going to raise a girl from the dead, and He got interrupted on the way. He stopped and did the necessary ministry. What more important apostolic miracle could you do than raising a girl from the dead? But He didn't rush by this opportunity, this interruption.

We've set up the structure of church to minimize interruptions, and to insulate ourselves from interruptions because we have a very important job that we must focus on.

But Jesus stopped and He engaged the interruptions. Jesus' style of leadership engaged with people. He didn't avoid people. He actually engaged with them.

I remember ministering with Dan Mohler for the first time. It was a shock to me, because I was standing there at two in the morning while he took time to pray for every single person at a thousand-person meeting. And I thought, "I've never seen a servant leader like this before."

He was modeling something that's different to me. I came from a church where we quickly needed to get you to the green room after preaching before you got mobbed. There are people that will try to suck your time, and they will try to pull on you.

But Dan Mohler said, "No, no, I can manage my own ministry." He said he could tell people when he had to go on to the next person, kindly.

Dan prayed for people until 2AM. I had to sit down, because I was tired, but he was standing up. It was so different than some of the other people that I've ministered with.

Jesus was constantly engaging and not avoiding people. Jesus also empowered people. There was no micromanagement in Jesus' style of leadership.

I was with a man named Larry in Saskatchewan who started *Street Invaders*, which is one of the most amazing youth ministries across Canada, where they empower young people to be the church. They are not waiting to be the church but taking ownership now. If you are thirteen years old, you're already too old for them.

The leadership in their church asked about a thirteen-year-old ministering. Was he old enough for this responsibility? Were they setting him up for failure? And the pastor said, "Yeah, you're right. He's probably too old."

I enjoyed my time with *Street Invaders* because they were trying to break down the paradigm of having a certain level of experience, where you had to sit under someone's covering so long before they released you.

Jesus sent 70 unlearned men out after a year of being with Him. When they returned, they were bragging about their anointing and their ministry. Jesus wasn't intimidated. He said, "Don't be excited and celebrate because of the signs and the wonders in your anointing and your ministry. Celebrate because you're in the Lamb's book of life."

He taught them to go out, make mistakes, cast out demons, heal the sick, do amazing things knowing that they had the power and the authority. Once they came back, He'd continue to teach them how to be humble, and how to serve.

In the church, we've constantly celebrated people's anointings and giftings and not celebrated because they knew how to be a lamb, who knew how to love.

We've seen that they could really lead because they're good communicators. But do they love people well? Do they love like Jesus loves?

We can teach them the skills, and we can add to the skills, but have we celebrated gifting above character? Jesus' model and standard for how people would know us is by our love, not how we grow ministry. It's by love.

Jesus demonstrated all these miracles, signs, and wonders. He raised the dead and then showed the disciples how to do it. He empowered them to do it. He said they'd go and do greater things than these. He constantly promoted and empowered His disciples. He wanted them to do greater things than He did.

True apostolic ministry is seeing disciples raised up and launched. We're still stuck in an old wineskin. If we're not careful, it can easily become a hierarchy or a pyramid scheme.

I've seen ministries where they have such big vision to see the world saved, to see cities saved, but it swallows up people's vision.

God has a vision that is specific for you, that will be a part of the body and that will serve the body, to see God glorified in the Earth.

Brian Simmons shared a story that really touched me. He was in the jungle with an unreached tribe. He and his family were living in the huts with the tribe, and the tribe was stealing from him constantly. The tribe was thinking, 'We can take advantage of these chumps that live with us. We can pretend to go along with them just to use them and to take from them." All of Brian's attempts to reach this tribe were failing. After a while, Brian said, "I can't continue to subject my wife to these kinds of conditions and this kind of abuse; I'm getting frustrated with these people."

He was getting bitter towards these people that he felt he was called to reach. He prayed, "God, everything I'm doing to reach these people isn't working. You called me here to this jungle to reach these people. What am I doing wrong?" God said, "I didn't call you to the struggle to reach these people. I called you to the struggle to reach you. And if I can reach you, I can reach the rest."

It broke his heart. He began weeping, realizing this was all about God reaching him. He felt so moved, he went to the next tent to repent to them. He started crying and weeping, telling them that he hadn't represented Jesus. "I'm sorry for not representing Jesus and loving you like you deserve to be loved." And they started shaking and feeling the presence of God, the power of God, and the Holy Spirit came and filled that hut. The whole family gave their lives to Jesus and the commotion caused people who were going out to work in the fields to come.

Within two weeks of repenting to every family, every family gave their lives to Jesus, and they had absolute, total revival because they had an experience with radical repentance. They just needed to be repented to and to be loved. The whole village was saved.

What Jesus said in Mark 10:35-45, was spoken right before He washed the disciples' feet. They were all arguing about who was the greatest. They didn't notice Jesus getting warm water and a cloth to wash their dirty feet.

While He was washing all their feet, He was modeling who was the greatest. Jesus demonstrated servanthood by washing their feet.

Questions for reflection:

Where have we failed to wash feet and instead expect that our feet be washed? How can we serve the people we lead?

Lesson 30 Bloom

Krysta Koppel

Every year, the Lord gives me a word or phrase that becomes a promise to hold onto, or an area to grow through. My word for 2023 was *bloom*. I love flowers, so immediately I thought about a beautiful bouquet of blooms, and I got excited thinking about what the bloom would look like.

As the year went on, I began to realize that the Lord had something else in mind because bloom is more than just a thing, a noun. It's also a process, an action, a verb. It began to dawn on me that process is what He wanted to take me through, and He began to speak to me about the process and journey of blooming.

The analogies between gardening and the Kingdom are as old as time. But it came more alive to me as I was working through a botany homeschooling unit with my kids. We explored the whole lifecycle of a plant and the journey that it takes to get a plant to flower; the place where we have this bouquet of flowers or potted plants in our house that blooms. It is a long journey. And it's easy to get so fixated on that end product that we forget what it takes to get there.

In 2024 as I was praying for this year's word, I felt like the Lord was saying, "Just keep going; continue to become grounded, rooted, and established. Most plants don't just produce one blossom, they continue to develop multiple blossoms.

One of my favorite flowers is the sunflower. I've always loved sunflowers. They're just so vibrant and beautiful. They are such a happy flower, in my opinion. I've been planting them for years. In my last house, we used to have a whole fence dedicated to sunflowers, and they were just spectacular.

Back to last summer, when I was taking my kids through the whole botany unit, we started with the sunflower seed. We dissected and examined the seed. The seed in itself is its own lesson because there's so much to it. Inside a small seed holds all the DNA for the plant. It holds all the initial nutrients it needs. There's so much potential just locked up in this tiny thing that frankly looks dead. It won't do anything until it's planted into the ground.

We planted some sunflower seeds along the south side of the house, but then we also planted some in a little plastic baggie with a wet paper towel so the kids could see the growth. It was fascinating. This is where I won them over on the botany unit because every day we could see new growth and we could actually see this seed germinate.

I tell you the truth, unless a kernel of wheat is planted in the soil and dies, it remains alone. But its death will produce many new kernels—a plentiful harvest of new lives. John 12:24 NLT

This made me wonder, does a seed actually die? It doesn't really, because it is very much alive; but it must be broken open, and the entire entity transforms.

Leadership Lessons from The Summit

When you look at a sunflower seed, you have no concept of what the sunflower is going to look like. The same with an apple seed or any other kind of seed. If you are handed an unlabeled seed, you will have no idea what plant or fruit it might produce until you put it in some soil.

The structure of the seed needs to die and, in its place, grows the plant that was meant to be. However, the breaking, the dying, can be painful.

There were some really painful moments that my family and I walked through from 2019 to 2022. But it was also freeing, and necessary for growth. I went through a time of stripping everything away, from career, relationships, ministry, things, even expectations and ideals that I had for my kids and my family, for my life, and my ministry.

So much of that had to be put aside and I had to come to the place where it was going to be okay; okay to just let it all go.

I think that's the place we all must come to.

Once a seed is planted and has germinated, then begins the development of its roots. This requires some form of soil, sun, water, and time before the shoot will break through the surface to sprout. There's so much that happens below the surface of the earth where the seed is planted that we're not even aware of. But it's essential for the growth of that flower to bloom.

My kids and I watched a time lapse video of a bean seed, and the root system underneath was double, triple, even quadruple the size of what the plant was. It's even more so for big trees. But it's fascinating to see the growth and development that happens, hidden, right in that secret place in that dark and cold. It's a place no one really wants to be, or chooses to be, but it's an essential part of the process.

Once the shoot starts breaking through the surface, there's so much growth and development that takes place in the plant as its stem grows, reaching various heights. You're waiting in anticipation for a flower. Sometimes it is a single flower, like a sunflower, but the stem is well over six feet tall, before a bud even begins to form. The roots don't ever stop growing either.

Finally, the time comes when the blossom opens. What we have been waiting for arrives in all its splendor. The flower is what we admire about a plant. It's often how we identify plants. There are so many unique and beautiful varieties. It's what birds, and bees, and pollinators are attracted to.

In a flower's life, there comes a time where it needs to produce fruit and seed. Like apples or watermelons or squash, the fruit is all produced to protect the seed, and all of them come from the flower.

In the case of my sunflower, it was filled with over 100 seeds with hard protective shells. Those seeds grew and developed, and as that happened, eventually the flower faded and died.

As much as we love flowers, they really don't last forever. A flower never thinks to itself, "I'm beginning to die." It's just part of the life cycle, part of the journey. You will never get fruit unless the flower dies.

We think that the beauty of a flower is the end game, the purpose, the goal, but it's not. It's the production of the seed. And there comes a point when the flower needs to give way to the fruit and the seed.

Then, of course, the whole process starts over again; as a seed goes to the ground, the cycle begins again.

Now, this whole blooming garden is not a new analogy, but it's one that I come back to time and time again. It's one where the Lord seems to always teach me something new.

As I moved into 2024, I had been focusing on this process and not the final product. I'm a linear thinker. Give me the product, give me the end goal, I will work towards that goal, and it'll be good. But sometimes, I just need to focus on the process. There are some lessons I am learning along the way.

First, the timing in the process matters. You can't force a plant to bloom at any time. It doesn't even matter what the weather or the conditions are like—you can have the perfect conditions, but the plant is going to bloom when it's ready to bloom.

For myself, it's an awareness of the season I'm in. Sometimes I am in a winter season, and it would be ridiculous to think that I am going to get a sunflower in the winter. I can wrack my brain, stress, and strive, wondering why this plant isn't growing, without recognizing what season I'm in.

In the winter, farmers take the time to rest. But they're also planning, and beginning to prepare, and thinking about what the next year is going to look like. It's a time of active waiting, learning how to wait, and learning how to rest but not necessarily to stop everything.

Other times, we're in seasons where there is active growth and there is a need to produce something. With the right conditions, it will come naturally.

When I can recognize the season that I'm in, there's less shame and there's less condemnation; there's a shift of expectation of what needs to happen.

The second thing that the Lord spoke to me about was to not put my roots down in something that's meant to be fruit. It's so easy to put our roots down in things like our professions, our talents, our abilities, our giftings, academics, and even relationships.

When we do, we settle for something that only brings temporary joy and peace. What happens when those things are gone? I chose to leave the profession of teaching in a traditional classroom setting, and that was a major shift for me. So much of my identity was wrapped up in what I did as a teacher. You can't put your roots down into something like that.

Then Christ will make his home in your hearts as you trust in him. Your roots will grow down into God's love and keep you strong. Ephesians 3:17 NLT

This is one of my life verses. It goes on to talk about the fullness of life and power that comes from knowing and loving God. This is the verse that I have held onto because there's nothing else that I needed to be rooted in other than His love.

I was looking back at some of the business goals I made over the past couple years, goals that I really felt the Lord was calling me to. If I tried to measure my business, my success by those goals, it was a complete failure. I was doing absolutely nothing with my business because the Lord asked me to pivot into a new assignment.

If my roots are in my business, then I determine my success and my failure, my worth, on that.

Instead, I want to be more rooted in God's love today than I was yesterday. That is be my measure of success; that's my plumb line: how deeply rooted I am in His love. And with that rootedness, what fruit am I producing? It won't matter what I'm doing as a job or ministry if my roots are in Him.

The third lesson is that we must be willing to let the blossom die for fruit to come forth. If we hold onto the flower, we'll never get the fruit that we really want to produce, which is the legacy of what's meant to come.

There's an old saying: you can easily count the seeds of an apple, but it's impossible to count the number of apples that are in a seed. The fruit is important because of the seed.

My final thought is back to sunflowers. One of the things I love so much about them is that they always face the sun. They track the sun; it's called *heliotropism*. As they begin to bloom, they'll move throughout the day; it's fun to watch. They will turn east in the morning and follow the sun; the head of the sunflower will follow it all the way to the west, and then overnight, it will turn itself back again in anticipation for the sun to rise the next day. Hence, the name *sunflower*.

It's such a beautiful picture of how we need to keep our gaze on the Son, Jesus. We need to move our face toward the Son and fix our gaze on Him. He is our source, our lifeline.

Questions for reflection:

Are your roots growing big enough to support your plant? What season are you in? How do you steward well the season you are in?

Lesson 31 Loyal Love

TJ Green

We use a lot of Bible Project materials in my house. They are a great resource and are very visual. Using Bible Project, I was reading the book of Ruth to my son, Dax, the other night.

The book of Ruth invites us to consider how God is involved in all the details, hardships and challenges of our lives. It's a beautiful story. It's like a piece of poetry, because you notice similarities at the beginning and at the end of each chapter.

In Hebrew writing, you're looking for symmetry, because it will show you something; it's weaving a story through all that symmetry.

The Passion Translation brings out the main theme of Ruth, which is loyal love. Other translations have simply translated it 'loyalty'. But loyal love is brought up multiple times in each chapter of this translation.

I am going to simplify the story for you. There's three main characters: Naomi the widow, Ruth the Moabite widow, and Boaz the Israelite farmer.

The scene opens with an important Israelite family, Elimelech and his wife, Naomi. It was a time of extreme famine, so they left Bethlehem, and went to enemy land.

It was to be easier there but still they had devastation, as all their sons died, and Naomi's husband, Elimelech, died too.

Ruth was left as a widow. With two pagan daughters-in-law, Naomi had no reason to stay. She told her daughters-in-law, "Don't come to Israel, because as a widow there is nothing for you. Also, being a pagan, you're going to be judged, you're going to be looked down upon. There's no place for you in Israel, so don't come."

But Ruth said, "I'm going where you go; your people will become my people. Your God will become my God." She showed incredible loyalty.

Naomi changed her own name to 'Mara', which means 'bitter'; the grief and the loss of her family had become her identity. She was in mourning and grief. When she and Ruth arrived in Israel, they wondered, "What are we going to do for food?"

It was the time for barley harvest. Ruth went out to look for food and ended up picking grain in the field of a man named Boaz.

Boaz was a relative of Naomi. Boaz heard a little about Ruth's story and her loyal love for Naomi by leaving her land to come where there was nothing for her. So, Boaz was very generous to Ruth.

Ruth came home, and told Naomi everything, and Naomi started freaking out because Boaz was her kinsman redeemer. In Hebrew culture, if there's a relative in the family, they must take care of the widows.

Naomi realized there was hope here. She thought her family was done. There was no lineage. Her history was over. Her story should have ended here.

Naomi started to have hope that maybe there was a story left for her family. Her family would be redeemed after all. So, Naomi and Ruth came up with a plan to attract Boaz. Ruth stopped wearing the grieving clothes to show that she was available.

Ruth approached Boaz, who was sleeping. She made her intentions very clear. "Will you redeem our family, Naomi's family, by marrying me?" Again, he was moved by Ruth's loyal love for Naomi.

Boaz said to wait until the next day, and he'd redeem both her and Naomi. The chapter ends with them marveling together at all that God was doing.

Boaz found out there was a family member who was closer, but this family member realized Ruth was a Moabite woman. He didn't want anything to do with her. He thought it was like bringing a curse, and he wasn't going to touch that.

But Boaz said, "No, she's a woman of noble character, loyal love." The story ends with justice. Ruth was loyal to Boaz. The story concludes with the reversal of all the death and tragedy.

It started out with the family in famine, dying, with no hope for their lineage to continue. It ended with a wedding and a birth of a son. The story ends with joy, and a new birth. The story theme is death that leads to new life, grieving that leads to joy, famine that leads to harvest.

This story is the picture of grief, and each chapter begins with Naomi and Ruth planning for their future; each chapter ends with them marveling or celebrating at what God is doing.

The interesting thing though, in the whole story of Ruth, is how little God is mentioned. He is not mentioned once by the narrator. It's not that He didn't do anything. There are prayers to God throughout the story, but it's one of the places in the Bible where God is not in the story. Or it seems like God is not in the story.

Because of God's providence and design, He worked behind every scene, weaving together circumstances and the choices of all these characters. This is a story of Providence. This is a story of God's hand behind the scenes that we don't always recognize.

Naomi thinks her tragedy is God punishing her, but the whole story is about God's mission to restore her and her family lines. This story explores this interplay of God's will and human decision.

I asked my son, Dax, questions after reading it to him. "What's the most interesting part of the story? He said, "Ruth being a gold digger."

What was the weirdest part? "Ruth uncovering his feet."

*"I am Ruth, your servant. Spread your **wings** over your servant, for you are a redeemer." Ruth 3:9 ESV*

The interesting thing is about that word *wings*, which is all through the Scripture.

*But for you who fear my name, the sun of righteousness shall rise with healing in its **wings**. Malachi 4:2a ESV*

*He will cover you with his pinions, and under his **wings** you will find refuge; his faithfulness is a shield and buckler. Psalm 91:4 ESV*

Wings, in Hebrew culture, is a reference to your cloak, which also speaks to your identity, what you are covered in, what you're dressed in.

In Matthew 9:21, when the woman grabbed onto the edge of Jesus' clothes, she was grabbing on to His identity as a healer. This was the prophesied Messiah, the son of David.

In Mark 10:50, Bartimaeus threw off his cloak that identified him as a beggar, so that he could be identified in something new.

Ruth's request to be covered under Boaz's wings was a request to be healed by him and identified with him, to be married, basically.

I asked Dax, "What was the most random part of the book of Ruth?" And he said, "The very last two Scriptures, it's just a list of names. Like, what's that about?"

It's a list of names; it's genealogy. I explained to Dax what our genealogy looks like in our family. Let's look at Biblical genealogy. King David was Boaz's great, great grandson. Boaz was in line for Jesus to come through his family line. Ruth was in the family lineage of Jesus. That's the beautiful part of her story.

Ruth's story is like every book in the Bible. It is pointing to Jesus and what God is doing behind the scenes. All our decisions and struggles in life point us to Jesus, and we're part of that story.

We're part of the genealogy. We are the sons and daughters of God because of Jesus. We're in that family, in that bloodline. So, we find ourselves in the book of Ruth being covered under His wings.

Question for reflection:

Where has God hidden Himself and been at work in the ordinary, the mundane decisions, and circumstances of your life?

Lesson 32 Season of Rebuilding

Nikki Mathis

I have been feeling we are in a season of rebuilding. We've come full circle from before COVID started.

When you think about the word "rebuilding", you rebuild something because it's been attacked. At Summit, we are not a culture that ever focuses on looking for the enemy or what he is doing. I don't like giving him credit for anything, but he exists.

During COVID, we opened a second location, as we felt like God was leading us to do that, but at the same time, we learned how that affected our culture, and how that was able to affect the unity and the growth of the church.

We are not trying to go back to January 2020 because we're never going to be that church again. When you go through changes and growth, you become stronger and wiser and have more maturity.

When I was reading Nehemiah, it stuck out to me when they were talking about rebuilding the wall; when Jerusalem's wall had been attacked, their gates had been burned down, and the wall had been attacked. Nehemiah really felt this passion to rebuild it.

But we prayed to our God and guarded the city day and night to protect ourselves. Then the people of Judah began to complain, "The workers are getting tired, and there is so much rubble to be moved. We will never be able to build the wall by ourselves." Meanwhile, our enemies were saying, "Before they know what's happening, we will swoop down on them and kill them and end their work." The Jews who lived near the enemy came and told us again and again, "They will come from all directions and attack us!" Nehemiah 4:9-12 NLT

I know you can find all these different parallels, symbols, and meanings in this passage, but I wanted to read it through the lens of being encouraged.

We are rebuilding and we are at a point where there is a lot of work to be done. There is a lot of intentionality in rebuilding ministries and rebuilding culture and re-teaching people how to worship.

We know the enemy can come in many ways: through offense, personal accusation, sickness, and so many other different ways.

So I placed armed guards behind the lowest parts of the wall in the exposed areas. I stationed the people to stand guard by families, armed with swords, spears, and bows. Then as I looked over the situation, I called together the nobles and the rest of the people and said to them, "Don't be afraid of the enemy! Remember the Lord, who is great and glorious, and fight for your brothers, your sons, your daughters, your wives, and your homes!" When our enemies heard that we knew of their plans and that God had frustrated them, we all returned to our work on the wall. But from then on, only half my men worked while the other half stood guard with spears, shields, bows, and coats of mail. The leaders stationed themselves behind the people of Judah who were building the wall. The laborers carried on their work with one hand supporting their load and one hand holding a weapon. All the builders had a sword belted to their side. The trumpeter stayed with me to sound the alarm. Nehemiah 8:13-18 NLT

I think it's cool that they were so determined and so passionate about rebuilding. I liked the description of the different ranks of people: there were armed guards who guarded the families, and they guarded the low parts of the wall where there were holes.

I thought it was interesting that there were men who were building the wall, and they had a sword on their sides. The labourers were there to clean the rubble and other tasks with one hand while the other hand was holding a weapon. The leaders were stationed behind the people who were building the wall, the labourers.

I can look at this and look at our ministry leaders, the people who we are building. Our culture carriers and the ones who are hands-on—they are moving rubble and rebuilding family and culture, and they're the ones that are putting their hands to the plow. We are the leaders who are there to station ourselves behind them and support them and guard them.

I like the fact that there was a trumpeter who would follow Nehemiah wherever he went. If he saw something, he would blow the trumpet and everyone was supposed to gather to where the trumpet was being blown, to come and fight together.

Then I explained to the nobles and officials and all the people, "The work is very spread out, and we are widely separated from each other along the wall. When you hear the blast of the trumpet, rush to wherever it is sounding. Then our God will fight for us!" We worked early and late, from sunrise to sunset. And half the men were always on guard. I also told everyone living outside the walls to stay in Jerusalem. That way they and their servants could help with guard duty at night and work during the day. During this time, none of us—not I, nor my relatives, nor my servants, nor the guards who were with me—ever took off our clothes. We carried our weapons with us at all times, even when we went for water. Nehemiah 4:19-23 NLT

Here are my takeaways from this.

First, in verse 14, it says, "Don't be afraid of the enemy. Remember the Lord who was great and glorious and fight for your families and homes." **Even in the small tasks, we need to keep our eyes on Jesus and stay in love with Him.**

In these years since COVID, we've stepped into a deeper revelation of beloved identity, knowing who God is, and knowing who He is in our lives. It really does cause us to fight from a different position where it's not about fear.

Even in the small tasks, even as we're making our preparations, we remember His goodness. We always will fight and operate from that place.

The second thing is to make sure the laborers and the builders are equipped with a weapon. Our founders, group leaders, volunteers, culture carriers—the ones who are labouring to establish vision and culture—need to know how to build and be ready to fight.

We are training them not to fight out of fear, but to fight from a place of beloved identity. We're training people to keep their eyes on Jesus.

I think that is the key for this season of warfare. Compared to ten years ago, the way that we all do warfare looks a lot different.

For example, I'm overseeing worship leaders, and I can see how each one of my leaders, the ones who are taking the steps and leading our congregation into worship, are different. Everybody is so vastly different. I saw a picture of each person having their own sword; some of them have a shield and different weapons in addition to their sword.

Our leaders and the people who are labouring in the church all carry a different weapon—they all have their own thing that is their weapon of defense.

Third, we need to be standing on guard, ready to blow the trumpet when we see the enemy coming to attack our builders. We must be watching and not have tunnel vision on what we're overseeing. We need to stand on guard for all of those people.

I think because we're going deeper in our own revelation of beloved identity, warfare doesn't come from a place of fear and worry. It comes from knowing that we're already victorious.

Now my beloved ones, I have saved these most important truths for last: Be supernaturally infused with strength through your life-union with the Lord Jesus. Stand victorious with the force of his explosive power flowing in and through you.

Put on God's complete set of armor provided for us, so that you will be protected as you fight against the evil strategies of the accuser! Your hand-to-hand combat is not with human beings, but with the highest principalities and authorities operating in rebellion under the heavenly realms. For they are a powerful class of demon-gods and evil spirits that hold this dark world in bondage. Because of this, you must wear all the armor that God provides so you're protected as you confront the slanderer, for you are destined for all things and will rise victorious.

Put on truth as a belt to strengthen you to stand in triumph. Put on holiness as the protective armor that covers your heart. Stand on your feet alert, then you'll always be ready to share the blessings of peace.

In every battle, take faith as your wrap-around shield, for it is able to extinguish the blazing arrows coming at you from the evil one! Embrace the power of salvation's full deliverance, like a helmet to protect your thoughts from lies. And take the mighty razor-sharp Spirit-sword of the spoken word of God.

Pray passionately in the Spirit, as you constantly intercede with every form of prayer at all times. Pray the blessings of God upon all his believers. And pray also that God's revelation would be released through me every time I preach the wonderful mystery of the hope-filled gospel. Yes, pray that I may preach the wonderful news of God's kingdom with bold freedom at every opportunity. Even though I am chained as a prisoner, I am his ambassador. Ephesians 6:10-20 TPT

We are being infused with this explosive power flowing in and through us to put on God's complete set of armour provided for us so that we will be protected as we fight against the evil strategies of the accuser. We would be stupid to think that the enemy doesn't have strategy to try to take out our church or try to take people out individually. It's still real.

In this mentality of standing on guard, we know that there is opposition, but we're still operating through peace. I appreciate that wonderful mystery. I feel like this is the response that we take as we stand on guard for what we're doing and what we're building: to pray passionately in the spirit.

The enemy does have strategies that are age-old, but we fight from the position of a victor. We mistake a message like this as if it is an old wineskin or it means we need to get an actual sword and do prophetic acts. Spiritual warfare in the past was always tied with dramatic screaming at the devil. But I don't believe that's what we're called to.

We still need the reminder that as we build, we build with more awareness because of what we have. I know I feel more on guard, wiser, and sharper to guard the ones who are building with me.

I am super encouraged and excited for what this year is going to look like as we rebuild stronger and healthier.

Around the Table

Questions for reflection:

What is your special weapon to fight with? As we are rebuilding the different ministries and leaders, what does it look like for you to stand on guard or be a watchman for them?

Lesson 33 Valuing One Another

Heather Paton

When Jesus had finished telling these stories and illustrations, he left that part of the country. He returned to Nazareth, his hometown. When he taught there in the synagogue, everyone was amazed and said, "Where does he get this wisdom and the power to do miracles?" Then they scoffed, "He's just the carpenter's son, and we know Mary, his mother, and his brothers—James, Joseph, Simon, and Judas. All his sisters live right here among us. Where did he learn all these things?" And they were deeply offended and refused to believe in him. Then Jesus told them, "A prophet is honored everywhere except in his own hometown and among his own family." And so he did only a few miracles there because of their unbelief. Matthew 13:53-59 NLT

I love that you can read through all the Gospels about who Jesus is. Everybody knew Him and talked about Him. The blind people would throw themselves in the street to be healed, and people were constantly yelling His name—losing their dignity, doing anything just to get around this man.

And yet, the people closest to Him took Him for granted and took His giftings for granted. In these verses, it doesn't say that He *wouldn't* do miracles, it says that He *couldn't*.

We have talked for years about trying to honour the people who surround us so that God's best is really pulled out of them. When we start to create a culture of familiarity, of commonality, we start to see people for their lack, what they don't bring to the table, or with what we wish they brought to the table.

We can do a disservice to God because He's put signs, wonders, miracles, and gifts in each and every one of us. If we don't see them, we do our church body a disservice. We do our city a disservice. We do Alberta, the nation of Canada, and everything we stand up and testify about a disservice. We do a huge disservice by looking at each other commonly, just as Jesus' brothers, sisters, and those who grew up in His hometown did.

I feel, as leaders, it's our job to see who God created the people we pastor to be, but it's also our job to do that with one another. We need to really honour and to see beyond the common tasks that we do and to see what's in each of us that we bring to the table. How is each one of us going to be used to alter the culture? How are we going to be used in our corner?

I think it was sad that so many of the people from Jesus' hometown were amazed by His teaching. They sat there in complete amazement thinking, "This guy is young; how does he know this? He's so smart. Where does he get this wisdom?" And then they turn around and totally dishonour Him. Jesus was not even able to do a miracle because of it.

Whenever we travel, people are waiting for us to come, because they know signs, wonders, and miracles are coming alongside us. They come with a spirit of expectation.

When we travel, our heart is to raise a country and to train countrymen to win the country. We want them to be empowered to do signs, wonders, and miracles themselves.

If they're looking at their leaders or their people commonly, then they're doing a disservice to the people who the Lord has put in their specific body.

We need to be cautious not to look at each other commonly and to not take each other for granted. My coworkers might be different from me, and they might bring something different to the table, but what they bring is what the Lord saw fit for the house.

It's like at a funeral when someone dies, people say all these great things about the person. The person who died would probably think, "I thought you hated me; you treated me terribly. You've never told me how much you loved me. You never really honoured me or seemed interested, so I left so much more on the table that could have been poured out."

People's gifts can be shut down because they think that they're not appreciated. Or they think that they're not valued. *"I'm not going to cast pearls before swine."*

Do you feel valued? Do you feel valued in your job? Do you feel valued in ministry? I'm not saying your value comes from other people, it should come from the Lord, but I think it's our job to champion one another and to really do what God's called us to do.

It goes beyond this table, to our teams, to the people who serve alongside us. Do they know that they're more than just the one who runs alongside us? Do they know that? They're the ones we really need, in their variety of talents and abilities. Do we honour those gifts in them and make sure that they feel seen and valued?

We can also be partnered with lies and so we can excuse ourselves from stepping out in something. For example, maybe someone else is praying for someone with my gift to step up, but I don't step up because I am partnered with the lie that my gift isn't valuable.

We play a part in seeing people as common or as miracle workers. We play a big part in calling people up and letting them know we think they are capable. It opens the door for them to step up and try.

When people feel, "I matter. I'm a part of this. I have gifts and talents," then everybody runs a little bit stronger. The entire Kingdom advances when we call out the gold in others. Let's call out the value we see in one another today and every day.

Questions for reflection:

What is it that you feel you can't do or haven't been able to do because you've been seen as common or familiar? What gifts do you see in those around you that you could call out?

Lesson 34 Pioneering and Church Growth

Chris Mathis

I love church planting. I love the idea of a family moving somewhere and starting something from scratch. It's wired in me, in my calling, and my DNA. Anytime I'm around people like that, it stirs me and brings life to me.

When you see what they're doing, you see things that inspire you and you see things that you wouldn't do. There definitely are some takeaways that I've learned.

A friend of mine was picking my brain about it, asking me a lot of questions because he was trying to go to the next level. He wanted to grow his church from 700 to 1,400. Don't we all? As the pastoral leader, he is doing so much himself.

I'm not used to running the way he runs. He has 6:30 am prayer every day at the church with fifty guys, which is awesome, then he goes to meeting after meeting after meeting all day. On Sunday, he has 6:30 am prayer, eats breakfast, has church service, takes his son to sports, goes back to church for the evening service, then eats dinner at 9:30 pm.

I told him that either he has got to be a machine, or he will run himself out. That opened some dialogue, and he was asking about our team.

I explained what my role is and what our team's role is. I encouraged him to empower other leaders around him to help. Not that he didn't already have leaders around him, but I encouraged him to take it further.

I believe our church is on the move. Awakening and revival is something we're constantly pressing into. We're seeing nations touched by the power of God, the gospel is being preached, and churches are being planted.

I keep coming back to being very careful not to settle, but to continue to have a pioneer focus and a building focus.

Church planting strategists teach that if a church does not reach 200 people in the first two years, it never will. I don't know if that's true or not. That's just what the church planting strategy says.

In my experience, we hit 200 people in the Summit Crestview during the third year, and I noticed after that it was really easy because when you experience a delay in growth, it's easy to enjoy it. Instead of going after what we need to do to maintain it and go to the next level, we can enjoy the process more.

I found that with church growth, pains come with it. And I think the pains that people felt were probably one of the key reasons why we experienced delayed growth. Not everybody wants the church to grow.

Growth always means change. Always. And change equals loss every time. You never have a change without some sort of loss.

Maybe it's one family, maybe it's ten families. Change always equals loss. There's no loss without pain. A church that wants to grow without going through pain is like a woman who says, "I want to have a baby, but I don't want to go through labour."

Is the pain worth it? Yes, in the end, it is always worth it. But how do we handle those pains? Rick Warren talks about the 'care issue'. Some of the people who have been around the longest will say, "The church doesn't care about me. Pastor, you really don't care about me anymore."

What this translates to when you hear that phrase is, "You're not available to me like you used to be when the church was small." They're right. I'm not available to every person.

When I moved to Edmonton, there were a lot of people who I was able to spend time hanging out with, going for lunches, and doing fellowships with. It's just not realistic in my life anymore. There are too many people pulling on me to meet with all of them.

I refuse to lead that way, running around trying to be the guy that is the connector for everyone in the church. It is just not realistic.

When people say that you're not available anymore, the solution isn't to double-down and work harder. The solution is small groups with secure leadership and a solid communication of the vision. Executing teams know how to implement and facilitate the family aspect in the church.

What does it mean when people say we have a 'care issue'? Are they saying, "You're not available to me?" Is it legitimate? If it is, let's figure out solutions. If it's not, let's figure out better language to communicate so that they're not so codependent.

There can also be a control issue when a church begins to grow. There are some people who say, "I don't feel as involved as I used to feel." Growth upsets the balance between the pioneers and the homesteaders.

As pastors, ministers, leaders, and people committed to the vision, we must be pioneers, not homesteaders. When a church begins to grow, there will always be criticism, and it must be avoided from within. Criticism cannot stick to us in a way that makes us react to it.

I'm not talking about healthy criticism. I'm talking about the criticism that says, "You are not providing for my needs anymore." Some of that can be legitimate on our leadership end, but I'm not talking about that. I'm talking about when the church begins to grow, when some people have the mindset where they get upset with the growth and they don't like the balance being upset between pioneers and homesteaders.

Pioneers are the people who have the grace to build and execute vision. Homesteaders just want to chill. "Let's put it on cruise control. This is great. I love church. And I loved it when the Pastor took me out all the time to play golf, and now, he doesn't anymore."

At first, when a church begins to grow, there's a lot of excitement. I remember the Sunday morning that the Paton's moved here. It was explosive. Probably about two years after that, we were going through a decline in attendance and people weren't showing up.

I was talking with Jamie, wondering what was up. He said, "It's no big deal; the honeymoon just wore off." That got me thinking. There is a honeymoon stage for people. It's important for us to not allow the honeymoon stage to ever end, just like in a marriage. It's our fault if we lose excitement. It's nobody else's. It's my fault if I lose excitement over my wife; it's not hers or anybody else's.

In the beginning, there was a lot of growth. It was great. We're part of something historic. Once you grow with more newcomers than established members, the common temptation is to ask the question: whose church is this?

We have people who came from the very beginning—the ones who are visionaries, the exciting ones, the passionate ones—and then suddenly, all these newcomers come, and the established people ask: whose church is this? The answer is that it's God's Church.

It's important that as the culture carriers, we don't let the newcomers override and dilute what God's doing in this church. We can have some measure of growth and some measure of control, but we cannot have a lot of control and a lot of growth at the same time.

As leaders, I think it's important for us to know that if we're trying to control every little detail, we're going to be miserable. We will run ourselves ragged, and that is not healthy.

Last is the comfort issue. We cannot grow without change and change is never comfortable. A lot of people want the church to grow as long as it doesn't make them uncomfortable.

If the church is continuing to grow, we must be willing to minister outside of our comfort zone. A good mindset to take in a growing church is to help establish new ministries. Start one, raise it up, hand it over to someone new, and then go start a new one and let the process continue.

The real issue is selfishness. It takes unselfish people in a community to grow the church. If we feel like we have taken ownership or control, that makes the church ours instead of God's. We must repent, and let it go.

If we feel like we have to corner the market on what we do, we're never going to equip the right leaders to do what they're called to do, which is replace us.

It allows us to move to something different and build something new. It doesn't mean we leave geographically. It just means we're growing a community. The church is a living organism, and we need to help it grow in a healthy way.

Questions for reflection:

Are you trying to do everything, or are you empowering others to lead? Where are you in the control/growth balance? How do you handle change?

Lesson 35 Mantles

Nikki Mathis

There are variations in the meaning of the word *mantle* in the Bible, but the main idea is covering, such as a cloak or an article of clothing. The NASB uses the word mantle in Joshua 7:21 and Hebrews 1:12.

In Joshua 7:21 the ESV translates the word as a cloak, and in Hebrews 1:12 as a robe. In Biblical times, a mantle was typically a large, loosely fitting garment, made of animal, probably sheepskin.

Several people are mentioned as wearing a mantle including Job and Ezra. Prophets were known for wearing mantles as a sign of their calling from God. The prophet Samuel wore a mantle, and the prophet Elijah threw his cloak around Elisha as a symbol of Elijah's ministry being passed on to Elisha.

The prophet's mantle was an indication of his authority and responsibility. As God's chosen spokesman, Elisha was not confused as to what Elijah was doing. The putting-on of his mantle made his election very clear.

Some theologians see the mantle as a symbol of the Holy Spirit. In 2 Kings 2:14, Elisha took the mantle that had fallen from Elijah, similar to how Jesus received the Spirit descending on Him at His baptism in Matthew 3:16. The audible voice of God in Matthew 3:17 confirmed Jesus as God's chosen servant. We see a similar falling of the Spirit in Acts 8:15-16 and Acts 10:44. After Elijah took the fallen mantle, he performed miraculous works.

The Holy Spirit is the person who empowers God's people to do God's work. The mantle served the practical purpose of keeping people warm and protecting them from the elements. It also served as a symbolic purpose in the case of the prophets showing that they were wrapped in God's authority.

Like all imagery in the Old Testament, the mantle presents a visible representation of a New Testament principle. Mantles can be seen as a symbol of the anointing of the Holy Spirit whom God so graciously gives to all Christians, the people of His choosing.

A mantle is a cloak of authority that you have been given. A mantle is given by God—not your pastor, not your leader or parents, not your music teacher or spouse.

We've talked about how people pray for their mantle to fall onto others. As much as we want it, that's just not how it works. Someone cannot pray that you receive it. Only God decides what mantles we receive.

This concept first came to me when we were in the Gulfstream Revival in the Florida Panhandle with Dutch Sheets in a little tent. Dutch, Chris and I, along with a couple of other leaders who were involved in that Gulfstream Revival were trying to decide who was going to be the leader of the worship.

Because there were churches coming together, each pastor wanted their person to be *the* worship leader. Dutch said something that has always stuck with me, "You need somebody who has a regional mantle to be able to carry a regional revival."

You could tell that there were some worship leaders who had the anointing for a small church, or a coffee shop feel, or they were mantled for their local church, but not necessarily for their city or for the region as a whole.

I accepted it because they asked me to be that person. It was as if the Lord was acknowledging through Dutch that I had a regional mantle for our region.

There are different kinds of mantles:

1. There is a local church mantle, which is the most common. They're reaching the people in their church, and they are assigned to that body and there's nothing wrong with that.

2. There is a citywide mantle. You will see people leading at citywide events, such as conferences with reach beyond their local church.

3. Regional mantles have an influence through their city and region and are recognized by other churches and leaders throughout the region.

4. National mantles have the reach throughout the nation and have influenced people from one side of the nation to the other.

5. International mantles have the mantle and influence to reach the world as a whole. You will see a high demand on those that carry an international mantle with invitations to lead worship.

All five mantles require intimacy with God, and all five mantles have a level of talent and ability that match the mantle.

I know that God can choose to re-mantle someone when His timing is right. This cannot be decided by anybody but God.

When you are young and you get words or prophecies that you are going to reach the nations, you assume that means an international mantle, and you start to chase that. You become dissatisfied when you're not doing it.

That's the discouragement that comes with prophetic words when people are not mature enough; it can hinder them instead of help them.

For me, the more influence I have, the more I don't want it. I look at all these ministries that are under the limelight and going through so much. I'm good with not having any more influence or getting any bigger. I'm fine with it. Because the bigger the mantle, or the more reach you have with your mantle, the more responsibility that comes along with it.

It's a lot of responsibility; you get a lot of critics, and you get a lot of people who will make videos about you and try to destroy your life and marriage.

The devil will try to come after you in relation to your size of mantle. There's an attack that's going to happen with anybody who has a large reach.

A larger size mantle can feel like an elevation or promotion. But ask anyone who has that mantle: it comes at a cost. The difficulties that come with that territory are large. However, God sustains those He mantles.

Those who make room for themselves will just be another dying star. There is no formula, process, or school that will fast track you. The process is specific to you and tailored for your life and the call that God has on it.

I've had worship leaders who tell me, "I'm called to lead worship. And I was the worship leader at my church for fifteen years, blah, blah, blah."

Then they want to come onto our platform, which has an international reach because of the people all over the world who are watching us and in community with us but also, more specifically, has national influence within Canada. The mantle on our platform is heavier than one that's coming from a local church.

Those worship leaders would then step on to our stage, because I want everyone to have opportunity, but they would buckle under the pressure. I found that a lot of times, they would leave the platform feeling discouraged, wondering if they were even called to lead worship, feeling like that was not who they were. It was too heavy for them to carry. It was too great a responsibility.

I teach our worship team that we need to understand that not everybody needs to be leading worship. There are some leaders who I tell, "I want you to grow. I want to protect you. I don't want you to be pushed into something that you're not ready for, something that can discourage you in the long run."

We are raising up leaders, and we must be able to look at the people we're leading and understand what they're mantled for and where they are right now. Even though we want to press people forward, to raise people up, we have to know they are ready. It can cause those who aren't mantled for it to buckle under the pressure.

The purpose in this is not to make your mantle your focus. The purpose is to focus on intimacy with God, loving Him and Him loving you, and to be content with that focus.

If you notice you're not operating in what you know you can carry, or you feel a sense of chaos, uneasiness, a lack of grace when leading, then you are leading outside your mantle.

The water level is rising. I'm seeing so much growth and promotion in the Spirit. When you receive more responsibility, it doesn't mean that you're better than others, it just means that you have more responsibility.

With a larger mantle, there is a greater responsibility to steward the atmosphere and the demand. Not everyone has the same level of gifting. Not everyone has the shoulders to carry certain things.

So regardless of what your gifting is, it's more about how broad your shoulders are to carry what you're carrying as we yield to the different seasons of battles.

It's important not to fall into jealousy, but to trust God that He has given you what you have the shoulders to handle. You need to understand what God has mantled you for, and what He has not mantled.

Questions for reflection:

When was a time that you wanted a different mantle than what God had given you? What do you know you are not mantled for right now?

Around the Table

Lesson 36 Church Leadership

Chris Mathis

The council members were astonished as they witnessed the bold courage of Peter and John, especially when they discovered that they were just ordinary men who had never had religious training. Then they began to understand the effect Jesus had on them simply by spending time with him. Acts 4:13 TPT

In the New King James Version, it says that Peter and John were ordinary, unlearned men. That word in the Greek is *idiots*.

They didn't go to Bethel Bible College. They didn't go to the University of Alberta. Council members began to understand the effect Jesus had on Peter and John simply by spending time with Him. That's profound to me.

The twelve apostles called a meeting of all the believers and told them, "It is not advantageous for us to be pulled away from the word of God to wait on tables. We want you to carefully select from among yourselves seven godly men. Make sure they are honorable, full of the Holy Spirit and wisdom, and we will give them the responsibility of this crucial ministry of serving. That will enable us to give our full attention to prayer and preaching the word of God." Acts 6:2-4 TPT

The church in the book of Acts was blowing up; it was full of life and excitement. People were getting saved left and right. But it also started to become internally focused.

We see this happen when they start arguing amongst themselves about who is waiting tables, who is doing more than the others, comparing themselves, and bickering.

We see later when Stephen gets stoned, a shift happens. That caused an outward focus. They go from internal focus to an outward focus. Why did that happen?

Persecution came from the outside. Boredom and internal self-serving brought internal conflict. Persecution from the outside will always bring growth.

But the more they afflicted them, the more they multiplied and grew. Exodus 1:23a NKJV

We should not hide from or avoid pain. It's pain that we should embrace because that's what multiplies and grows us.

The church here is apostolic and prophetic in nature. 'Apostolic and prophetic' is not just a stream in the church. It's a foundation of the church, built on the apostles and prophets, with Jesus Christ being the chief cornerstone.

I want us to understand this because we are an apostolic people. We're a prophetic people. It's not just a stream in the church. It doesn't mean we're all apostles. It means we're apostolic and prophetic in nature.

So, what does that look like? Stephen was one of these men chosen in Acts 6 to take the role of being a dishwasher, a cleaner, and server. That's what his role was in the church, a cleaner of dishes and server of the people.

I love this because he did not let his job description limit his anointing. If the church would get this, we would be so much more effective, profound, and even relevant. A lot of people don't take the church seriously because we are position driven and title driven.

Stephen was serving people in the church, and for part of that time, he was venturing outside without any church notoriety. He was healing the sick, raising the dead, and yet, he was a dishwasher.

The standard for New Testament Christianity is not that the apostle who is highly visible moves into power; the apostle is actually the lowest on the totem pole.

How do we walk in this apostolic grace?

First, connection, submission, and impartation. Connection is vital--connection at this leadership table and with the people in this body. Submission to the Lord is also important along with impartation from the Lord and from leaders.

Second, is faithfulness and steadiness. What impresses me is not somebody getting on fire on a Sunday. The real question is: 25 years down the road, are they still on fire? Faithfulness is the pathway.

Third, is confident leadership. Confident leaders don't just kill the giants. They let other people kill them too. They don't just run after the thing that's going to get them fame and glory. They're happy to pass it on to someone else, and let others achieve the praise. You see this with David and his mighty men.

Fourth, is empowering culture. Empowerment calls out the gold in you and turns you loose. The apostles did not lose heart. They didn't get jealous. They didn't become insecure. When they were hearing the rumours of Stephen healing the lame, they didn't shut it down. They didn't say they needed to be present, but instead empowered others.

I've served under insecure leaders where I've felt like I couldn't do anything. It had to be done through their word with them being present. Those kinds of cultures are really stifled; they don't grow. People don't feel empowered. Eventually in the long term, people won't stay, and if they do, you have to manipulate them to stay.

Fifth, is a submitted heart. I love this about apostolic cultures. This is really what they're called to do. They're called to function in a breaker anointing. What is a breaker? It is anointing to break off strongholds, to break through mindsets that have controlled people and atmospheres. It is the power of God manifesting a path for people to walk in freedom. That's what a breaker anointing does.

And everyone can function in this. The only limits we will experience is when this breaker anointing only operates in a leadership team.

Our goal is to empower people in the church to function. We don't want it to just function through this team. We want it to function through everybody in our culture.

A couple of keys to a breaker anointing:

1. Don't wait for someone else. Questions you can ask yourself are: if everyone was worshiping like me, how would the worship service be? If everyone prayed like me, what would our prayer culture look like? If everyone gave like me, what would our generosity look like?

   We have some forbidden phrases here. We won't say, "Our church doesn't _____." For example, our church doesn't give. Our church doesn't have children's volunteers, our church doesn't press into God, etc. The Lord said to stop saying that about the culture. The right phrase is, "I have not led them to _____." It shifts the responsibility off the people and puts it on those in leadership.

   Because as leaders, our job is to lead people, so if there is no breakthrough happening, what's missing? If people in the congregation aren't getting it, how do we lead them into it? Instead of getting frustrated and projecting the blame back on them, we need to lead them into those things.

   We need to teach people how to respond in a moment, in an environment, or in an atmosphere.

2. Don't try to impress. Aim at being faithful, not profound.

3. Do not distort honour. What does this mean? Flattery for the sake of your own promotion is not honour.

4. Don't allow a distraction of mood, argument, or temporary circumstance to impair your boldness in the moment.

5. Let God worry about your legacy.

These are some of the ways that we lead here. We believe in apostolic and prophetic leadership of the church; we believe in the five-fold ministry. As the leaders of the church, we are accountable to God in all we do, so we want to lead well.

Questions for reflection:

Do you lead like Stephen? Which apostolic grace do you struggle with? Do you walk in breaker anointing?

Leadership Lessons from The Summit

Other Books by
Summit Global Publishing Ltd.

Living in Devotion

A 40-day devotional book by The Summit Edmonton Church

Signs, Wonders, Miracles:

Testimonies from The Summit Volume 1

Signs, Wonders, Miracles:

Volume 2

Summit Global Publishing Ltd.

In December 2020, Tracy Belford received a vision from the Lord to open a publishing company. The purpose was to share the word of the Lord that was coming out of The Summit Edmonton Church. She was inspired by Romans 10:17 (NKJV) *"So then faith comes by hearing, and hearing by the word of God."*

Tracy believed that God was sharing so much wisdom and revelation within her church that it needed to be shared on a larger scale to increase the faith of many. To date, she has published several books:

Wise Money: Biblical Wisdom for Budgeting, Saving, Credit, and Giving

1st Habit of Wisdom: Revere the Lord

Signs, Wonders, Miracles Volume 2

Signs, Wonders, Miracles: Testimonies from the Summit Volume 1

Living in Devotion: 40 Day Devotional

Month of Captivation: Prayer Journal 2025

Hope for the Broken Soul

Leadership Lessons from The Summit

www.ingramcontent.com/pod-product-compliance
Lightning Source LLC
Chambersburg PA
CBHW071113160426
43196CB00013B/2558